Praise for THE

"Greg Kaplan's *The Journey* ref
stressful college application process into a powerful jou
self-discovery, authenticity, and leadership development."

—MATTHEW BREITFELDER, Partner and Global Head of
Human Capital, Apollo Global Management

"*The Journey* helps parents find the right balance between
support and independence as their children apply to college and
explore future career paths. This book provides excellent
advice not only for the college application process but
for the broader context of life."

—BARBARA HEWITT, Executive Director, Career
Services at the University of Pennsylvania

"Wow, *The Journey* really hits the nail on the head! Realistic,
filled with honesty and firsthand experience dealing with college
counseling for both student and parent. Eye-opening and truthful
about what college admission officers are looking for in a high
school senior applying to college in today's world with true grit,
passion, and leadership. As someone who works with stressed-out
high school seniors and their overly anxious parents, I especially
appreciate the ideas discussed in this book that are informative,
insightful, hopeful, and valuable concepts that hit home. A
must-read for college-bound students and their parents in
this overly very competitive college and career world!"

—MARY RUSSELL, college and career counselor for
Newport Mesa Unified School District

"I have been shocked by how intensely competitive and unhealthy the college admissions process has become, akin to the stress of applying to medical school. Through 20 years of training medical students, residents and rheumatology fellows, the recipe for success distills down to loving what you do and working hard. Being a firm believer in wanting my kids to be the *best* version of themselves and follow their passion, I tried to stay clear from the college counselor frenzy. It wasn't until halfway through my daughter's junior year that I met Greg Kaplan, and finally found someone who was like-minded. Greg's book is truly a gem, urging a much-needed realignment of how we and society define success. All parents and students should read this book as they embark on the process. It will help them focus on curating a growth mindset while focusing on building grit, cultivating passion, and becoming a leader. In my opinion, these are the most important gifts we can give to our children that will prove invaluable throughout their life."

—SHEETAL B. DESAI, MD MSEd, clinical professor and
Chief of Rheumatology, University of California, Irvine

The

JOURNEY

HOW TO PREPARE KIDS FOR A COMPETITIVE AND CHANGING WORLD

Greg Kaplan

Health Communications, Inc.
Boca Raton, Florida

www.hcibooks.com

Library of Congress Cataloging-in-Publication Data

Kaplan, Greg, author.

The journey: how to prepare kids for a competitive and changing
world / by Greg Kaplan.

Boca Raton, FL: Health Communications, Inc., [2024]

LCCN 2023050682 (print) | LCCN 2023050683 (ebook) |
ISBN-13: 9780757325045 (paperback)
ISBN-10: 0757325041 (paperback)
ISBN-13: 9780757325052 (epub)
ISBN-10: 075732505X (epub)

LCSH: Parenting. | Children--Vocational guidance.

LCC HQ755.8 .K353 2024 (print) | LCC HQ755.8 (ebook) |
DDC 649/.1--dc23/eng/20231108

LC record available at https://lccn.loc.gov/2023050682
LC ebook record available at https://lccn.loc.gov/2023050683

Publisher: Health Communications, Inc.
   301 Crawford Blvd., Suite 200
   Boca Raton, FL 33432-3762

Cover, illustrations, interior design, and formatting by Larissa Hise Henoch.

To my students:
Make the most of your journey.

TABLE OF CONTENTS

● ● ●

INTRODUCTION

• • •

> DON'T ASK WHAT THE WORLD NEEDS.
> ASK WHAT MAKES YOU COME ALIVE AND GO DO IT.
> BECAUSE WHAT THE WORLD NEEDS IS
> PEOPLE WHO HAVE COME ALIVE.
>
> —BRENÉ BROWN

QUESTION: Where do you see yourself in ten years?

ANSWER: (1) Financially stable, and (2) happy.

THIS IS THE FIRST QUESTION I ask when meeting new students, and since it is seemingly unrelated to college, it catches them off guard. Believe it or not, based on answers from the thousands of high school students I meet, the heartfelt desires of the next generation are relatively simple. They want to have a stable career, and they want that career, among other things, to make them happy.

Yet at the end of the day, this simple good is all we can want for ourselves or our children. And it is why elite universities are so coveted by students and parents alike. What parent doesn't want their child to be successful? What child doesn't see themselves living independently as an adult? And isn't it easy to assume that the path to success is through a name-brand university and a prestigious career?

While it is comforting to see young people being mindful of the importance of their health and financial independence, their underlying concern for their futures at the core of their answers initially caught me by surprise. Is it too much to ask for today?

Young people today are coming of age amid intense economic uncertainty. When I was sixteen, most of my peers assumed that they would eventually become successful. But our failure to launch has proven that we can no longer assume that financial stability or happiness is a given. A study by Credit Karma found that 40 percent of millennials and Gen Zers rely on their parents for financial support, while the Centers for Disease Control and Prevention reported that a whopping 20 percent of teen girls in the United States grapple with depression.

All these horrifying statistics stem from the same root cause: Young people are uncertain about their path in the world and feel the stress of being possibly unable to reach their goals. More often than not, this stress manifests itself in an unhealthy attitude toward college applications, a process often seen as the culmination and ultimate assessment of a young student's accomplishments and promise.

As a college counselor, I am often confronted with dark emotions that suggest that the students I work with are not prepared to seize the day. The following is an example of what happens too often in my office:

"My life is over."

A high school senior, Chloe, was in my office and sobbing. Wiping her eyes, she asked, "What's the point of even trying anymore?"

I was speechless.

Had she just been diagnosed with an incurable disease? No. She was a model of physical health. A survivor of a natural disaster? Had I unwittingly triggered her PTSD? Nope. Her childhood home remained firmly standing behind an imposing guarded gate. Had she just been informed of the passing of a beloved? Possibly a parent? Again, no. Her mother, Nora, was sitting beside her, trying to process whatever it was that left them distraught. Her father, out of town on a business trip, shared their distress via FaceTime.

So, what was it?

This scene happens over and over in April when colleges announce their admissions decisions for their incoming fall classes. However, I never expected to face it so often. Despite all its flaws, at its core, the college admissions process measures an applicant's growth in high school and potential to apply it to higher education.

I wrote my first book, *Earning Admission: Real Strategies for Getting into Highly Selective Colleges*, as I was first starting out as a private college admissions counselor. A road map to maximizing college acceptance potential, *Earning Admission* ended on an optimistic note urging parents and students alike to be excited about the college admissions process.

Seven years later, I've helped thousands of students prepare for and make the most of the college application process. Along the way, I have seen genuine passion, natural talent, and intense drive. Many of these students were admitted to their dream schools, including highly selective universities like Yale, Stanford, and UCLA. Even for those who were not admitted to their dream schools, I was still excited. I saw limitless potential in their futures because, even though the college process hadn't gone exactly their way, they had grown and were prepared to make their mark on the world.

I've also met countless parents with a healthy approach to fostering their kids' growth. They ably balance guiding and advising their children without being overbearing. They set realistic expectations and prioritize their children's health and happiness above all else. They hold their kids accountable and admonish and teach them when appropriate. Most importantly, they empower their children to form and chase their own dreams.

But despite their best intentions, not every parent falls into this category. Sometimes parents unwittingly do more harm than good when they fight every battle for their children, or blindly chase prestigious school names over relevant skills and perspectives that their kids will need to succeed.

That's what happened with Chloe, who declared that her life was over because she was rejected from Stanford. Let me put that into perspective for you: after factoring in legacy applicants and athletic recruits, Stanford rejects close to 99 percent of its applicants, including those with perfect grades, college entrance exams, and résumés.

Sitting beside her sobbing daughter, Nora turned to me and, with a businesslike shake of her head, began making excuses. The first excuse she thought of was the university was racist. I didn't know what to say to her. Over a quarter of the school shared the same ethnic background as her daughter. Would it be possible to speak to the university? No, I said; college admissions offices don't offer meetings to explain each decision they make.

Sensing that she was backed into a corner, Nora wondered aloud: Maybe her high school had sabotaged her daughter because she'd complained about two teachers who gave her daughter a B in her college-level calculus class. Could she speak to her lawyer about suing the school? Perhaps, I said, but high schools want to see their students have success in the college admissions process because it reflects well on them, so that possibility was highly unlikely.

Having exhausted all her options, this mom came up with one final strategy. It was okay. Chloe would reapply the following year and she would surely be admitted then: which is precisely what needed to happen so that Chloe could grow up to be a tech entrepreneur.

I didn't know what to say to either of them. Yes, it is normal to be disappointed by a college rejection, but this was not just a clear overreaction but a misguided belief of what was needed for Chloe to be prepared to achieve her long-term goals.

Yet, as a private college counselor, I can't make this stuff up. I wonder: *Are we doing enough to prepare our children for the next steps of their lives in a rapidly changing, hypercompetitive world?* If you need a minute to think, don't worry. You're not alone. But let's start with the prime example of what we shouldn't be doing.

In 2019, in a nationally explosive scandal dubbed "Operation Varsity Blues," Newport Beach, California–based college counselor Rick Singer was charged with federal racketeering and wire fraud for developing an admissions scheme in which wealthy families paid bribes to facilitate their children's admission to highly selective colleges.

The explosive publicizing of this scandal exposed the great lengths many parents go to in order to "help" their children. These methods, previously whispered about privately in affluent areas, were laid bare for the world to see. As a college admissions adviser with a practice in Newport Beach, the scandal hit too close to home for me. I had heard of Rick Singer in the community, and I was angry. I was convinced that it was the end of my career advising students in a healthy and honest way. But I wasn't the least bit surprised.

A *Los Angeles Times* reporter called me the morning that the U.S. Attorney announced the indictments against dozens of families and asked if I could comment on the story. *Of course I could*, I thought. Do I tailor my response to just Singer's actions and lay the blame solely on him? Or do I tell the truth about what is really going on with the college admissions craze?

Holding true to my desire to help students grow and achieve their dreams, I chose the latter. Despite my fears that it would turn away existing and potential clients of mine, I told the reporter that the Varsity Blues scandal was not news. It was a symptom of a larger societal problem that extended past the college counseling industry: a toxic approach to parenting that is devouring many young, promising lives.

I let the reporter know, on the record, that the parents who hired Singer were as much to blame as he was. Getting into Stanford, Georgetown, or an Ivy League university has evolved into the ultimate status symbol. It requires the perfect combination of financial resources, parental success, and natural student aptitude. College admissions have become the modern-day gold rush for many high-achieving communities and a chance for parents to show that beyond being successful in their own lives, they have also succeeded in raising equally promising children. For parents desperate to strike gold, Singer's approach to college admissions struck a chord.

The reporter wanted to know what it would take to prevent

something like this from happening again. Better regulations? More transparency with how admission is decided? A different approach to college admissions entirely? I told her that all those would be nice, but we need to go back to where it all begins: at home.

To make this process healthier and more rewarding for our children, we need to change the way we think about college in general. Getting into a good college is important, but college is the means to an end, not the be-all and end-all. A college education is a chance for students to develop the skills, perspective, and experience they need to achieve their long-term career and life goals.

Yet, many parents have lost sight of this as they zero in on the shininess of college names that sound amazing: Harvard, Stanford, MIT. This mindset affects every parenting decision they make. For the reporter, I cited mad spring dashes to enroll in overpriced summer camps hosted at fancy colleges or how parents threaten to sue teachers and schools when their kids earn Bs on essays that the parents wrote. The reporter was shocked. She had a two-year-old at home and was dumbfounded that this was what awaited her when her child reached high school.

As a society, we are seeing more than just wealthy adults bribing elite universities and hiring people to help students cheat their way into college. We are seeing crippling mental health issues in teens and young adults that are exacerbated by the pressure to perform at the highest levels. We are seeing a proliferation of cheating, sometimes sanctioned by parents, to maintain those high levels of performance. And when kids are admitted to college, even their dream schools, we see the true damage of these habits. A whopping 55 percent of Yale undergraduate students surveyed in a study confessed to being chronically depressed. Ill-prepared for the real world, 43 percent of college students are now dropping out or are unable to finish their degrees within six years of starting their college studies.

My *LA Times* interview, which I expected to potentially make me unappealing to existing and prospective clients, was distilled into a small quote about a status obsession. Meanwhile, my business continued to grow at an unprecedented rate, held aloft by college acceptance rates that continue to plummet to new lows. Families, terrified that they are being left behind in the college admissions frenzy and challenging job market, continue to hire me. The irony is that, if anything, the Rick Singer scandal made people today even more concerned about their kids' odds of earning admission to highly selective colleges and even more willing to seek professional help.

Everything that didn't make it into the *LA Times* article is discussed in this book. But beyond the college obsession held by many, I want to orient the conversation to how best to prepare one's kids for a changing and competitive world so that they can achieve health, happiness, and financial independence—which means we need to ask ourselves: Where is our shortsighted obsession with achievement leading us?

If you don't believe me, just look at the stats. Twenty-five percent of young adults ages twenty-five to thirty-four are unable to afford to live away from their parents.[1] We are on the precipice of millions of white-collar jobs evaporating due to technological advancements like artificial intelligence. At the same time, business leaders and employers are raising red flags that the biggest threat to the survival of their businesses is their ability to attract and retain qualified workers. Beyond these statistics, I can give you firsthand anecdotal evidence, straight from my college counseling offices, of kids who are about to crack when they encounter the harsh real world because they are unprepared to face it head-on.

So, what should parents be doing to prepare their kids for the world they are inheriting?

Every child is on a unique path to achieving their version of fulfillment. What makes them tick will shape what they need to do to achieve their goals. With that said, here are three key traits that parents should help their children cultivate for their futures that, oddly enough, are also exactly what college admissions officers look for in prospective students:

1. Grit

Grit is defined as one's ability to deal with life's monumental and day-to-day challenges. In an era when young people are dropping out of college over roommate disagreements and dining hall food not to their liking, or increasingly relying on their parents to address concerns with their bosses at work, instilling grit in the next generation is critical. While sports can help young people grow physically and mentally stronger on a field, court, or in the pool, we need to prepare young people for all aspects of their lives.

Yet sometimes parents prevent their children from developing grit by being *snowplow parents*. Like any strong herding dog (think German shepherds, Australian cattle dogs, border collies, etc.), snowplow parents dedicate themselves to removing every obstacle from their child's path. This is done not to ensure survival but rather achievement. By doing so, they prevent their child from developing the critical skills they need to independently overcome obstacles and thrive.

Other times, parents transform into *terminator parents*. Similar to the fiercest rottweilers or mastiffs and related to the snowplow parent, these parents will stop at nothing and engage in scorched-earth tactics to ensure that their child achieves what the parents want them to. Whether it is threatening to sue a school or teacher over an undesirable grade or finding doctors who corroborate learning differences to get extended time on college entrance exams, the terminator parent who will stop at nothing goes to great lengths to achieve potentially Pyrrhic victories. Along the way, they set a dangerous precedent for their child that achievement at all costs is worth it.

Instead, to instill grit in young people, we need to make sure they know what it's like to be the low person on the totem pole and deal with a difficult boss, coworkers they don't like, and customers who make them want to pull out their hair. Said differently, we need to make sure teens obtain a part-time job so that they can learn how to diffuse World War III when they put the wrong milk in a latte. Through these experiences, they will learn how to deal with difficult situations outside their control and recognize how hard they will have to work to achieve their goals. They will learn to appreciate what an incredible opportunity it is to chase their dreams through college and career and hopefully make the most of it.

2. Leadership

Colleges and employers alike seek applicants who can propel their organizations forward and change them for the better. They seek applicants with initiative and the ability to bring their peers and colleagues together to achieve a common goal. They seek leaders capable of making an impact. In today's competitive and tomorrow's even more competitive world, individuals who can apply their perspective and skills will be rewarded with opportunities to advance and grow through their education and careers.

But parents who get complacent and believe that their child is God's gift to the world miss out on opportunities to help their child develop the necessary leadership skills to make an impact on that world. One example of this is the *entitled parent*: the parent who has to have their cake and eat it too. This parent teaches their child that the world revolves around them. The end result is similar to a teacup yorkie or maltipoo that is bred to fit in a small handbag to elicit *oohs* and *aahs* at a high-end shopping mall but is unable to fend for itself in the wild. This parent can hinder their child's ability to actually make something of themselves because they raise their child to expect things from the world rather than contribute to it.

Other times, *special snowflake parents*, as the term suggests, treat their children like unique, precious, and one-of-a-kind snowflakes. One of the most common parent archetypes out there, these parents are under the mistaken belief that whatever their child does is special not just to them or their family but to the whole world. Just like how all snowflakes are unique in their own way, all children are special to their parents in their own unique way. The problems arise when special snowflake parents try to carry this logic to how the rest of the world sees their child. Special snowflake parents may seek to insulate their snowflakes from reality and as a result make them ill prepared to navigate the real world.

Leadership doesn't come easily or naturally for any of us. Rather than chasing empty titles and résumé fluff, parents should encourage their children to learn how to analyze situations to find ways to improve them, lead others, and form constructive relationships that benefit all.

3. Passion

Passion is the North Star that should guide a young person to
unlock their full potential and build a rewarding life. There are
no right or wrong careers to pursue or fields to study. While
some are more economically viable than others, young people
will find success at the intersection of what they enjoy, what
they excel at, and where there is a market opportunity. We
need to be honest with ourselves. In some fields, like the arts, it
may be hard to sustain oneself on passion alone. But there are
opportunities to apply what the arts can channel—creativity—
to other fields (for example, creating a brand image as a marketing professional, making arguments as a lawyer, designing
products as an engineer, or designing homes as an architect).

Yet, many parents often mistake impressive labels for passion, or worse, make collecting accolades their passion, which
in and of itself is not sustainable. These parents include the
label tyrants. While many dog parents place a premium on
AKC thoroughbred breeds and are willing to pay top dollar for
strong lineages despite the fact that purebred dogs are at a risk
for serious health issues and complications due to their limited gene pools, label tyrants place an emphasis on the labels
affixed to their children's development, often at the expense of
their children's development as people. By prioritizing name
brands over growth, label tyrants prioritize status, which can
encourage children to tie self-worth to a narrow range of
achievements—which in turn contributes to their anxiety
levels.

Meanwhile, *sports-crazed parents* do the same thing but
with an unrealistic emphasis on sports. Like a Labrador re-
triever who wants to swim, play catch, and stay as active as

possible, a sports-crazed parent views athletic achievement as supreme over all other forms of their child's growth. While sports can contribute to anyone's development, a sports-crazed parent is prone to promote athletic development at the expense of other facets of their child's growth, including their academics and other potential passions off the field or court. Often, under the mistaken belief that sports are their child's path to college, sports-obsessed parents place all the eggs in the sports basket and may be left holding the bag when their child is not one of the 7 percent of high school athletes recruited to play a sport in college[2] or the paltry 2 percent that receive any form of an athletic scholarship to help pay for college.[3]

Rather than orienting the conversation around achievement, we should orient our kids toward the journey to discover, develop, and evolve their passions, so that they can find fulfilling careers that reward their skill sets.

This book provides prescriptive advice to parents and students alike. Each part of the book includes a chapter on what parents can do to help prepare their children to make the most of the opportunities they will encounter in life. In the spirit of empowering young people with agency to take ownership of their lives, each part also includes a chapter written directly to young people, so that they can incorporate the guidance into their lives. Young people and their parents are on the same team in this journey, and I hope that this format encourages families to work together in healthy ways to prepare their children for the next steps.

Since the Varsity Blues college admissions scandal, I have worked with many more students, and my experiences have only strengthened my belief that the college admissions process is not just about earning admission to selective colleges. Rather, we must be intentional in helping the next generation develop grit, leadership, and passion. And as a college admissions counselor, my job is not just to help kids get into college. My job is to help them find their passions, gain meaningful experiences, learn how to reflect upon their growth and ability to contribute value to an organization like a college, and guide them toward a path that makes sense for their future goals.

Young people today are facing a perfect storm of skyrocketing tuition costs, plummeting college acceptance rates, and a seismic shift in the labor market that makes it incredibly difficult for new graduates to achieve financial independence as young adults. Parenting in the modern world is challenging, and there is no manual to follow. The biggest gift parents can give their children is a foundation to become independent young adults who are equipped to make their mark on the world.

For the college counseling industry, the confluence of factors at play demands that we reorient our mindset and start a healthier conversation about how an education can help students reach their long-term goals. Parents must make a concerted effort to avoid toxic behaviors that hinder their child from becoming a healthy, happy, and financially independent adult. Regardless of the role you play in the village that raises a child, each of us must be cognizant of our behavior and approach to preparing students for their future. For the next generation, this is an exciting time. Endless possibilities and opportunities await them. It is up to us to ensure that they are able to seize their opportunity when the time comes. This book is a tribute to the journey it takes to raise the next generation and our hope that we will prepare them for their own journey into college, adulthood, and beyond.

Part 1

GRIT

IT ALWAYS SEEMS
IMPOSSIBLE UNTIL IT IS DONE.

—NELSON MANDELA

CHAPTER 1

Grit Pushes the World Forward

DEFINING TRAITS OF THE CHILD WITH GRIT: *Grit, as a personal trait, is sustained enthusiasm and persistence for long-term goals.*[4] *Those who possess grit are able to self-regulate and postpone their need for positive reinforcement while working on a task. Grit is stick-to-itiveness, a diligent spirit, the nagging conviction that keeps one pressing on when it'd be easier to give up, and the ability to frame obstacles as growth challenges.*

BEHAVIOR PATTERNS: *Grit includes having the fortitude not to quit before reaching one's goal, regardless of how difficult it may get. A person with grit is able to remain constant and deal with the world's problems that are outside their control and not let those issues interfere with what needs to be done. Grit is what makes someone climb back on a bike when they have fallen off and continue on to reach their destination. Grit manifests itself when realizing that achieving one's greatest potential comes from running a marathon, not a sprint.*

WE LIVE IN AN ERA THAT IS DEFINED BY ITS COMFORT. Hungry? Do not fret, as no toiling in the kitchen (ugh) or schlepping to a restaurant (sigh) is necessary. We can remain comfortably on our couch and wait for an online order of gourmet food that is just a click away. While waiting for said food to be delivered to our doors, we can remain relaxed in clothing designed to be comfortable rather than stylish or attractive, especially as the business casual and formal clothing we were accustomed to wearing to work or seeing friends has been replaced by a permanent wardrobe of sweatpants, leggings, slippers, and sandals. Even other inconveniences like walking our dogs can be outsourced to apps designed to make our lives easier and more comfortable. But along the way, we may have become too comfortable with prioritizing our comfort. It's not just that we no longer have to bother learning to cook when we can order through DoorDash, drive when we can call an Uber, or exercise Fido when we use Wag. It's about something more: sticking with a task, even when it may feel more convenient to quit in the moment.

We need to be comfortable with being uncomfortable because sometimes that is what it takes to reach our goals and find satisfaction with our lives. With mental health finally receiving the attention it deserves, researchers have been turning their attention to the factors that can contribute to it. For example, studies show that individuals with high levels of grit are more likely to be inspired to achieve their life goals and pursue the meaning of life.[5] Perhaps this is why grit is of great significance to college students' growth and can bolster them to pursue and achieve their life goals through effort even when they face adversity, all while improving their life satisfaction in the process. Previous research has shown that grit is positively correlated with life satisfaction, and individuals with higher grit also have higher life satisfaction.[6]

Our formative years can be the most uncomfortable. The same is true when we are new to something or learning a new skill or hobby. The joy of doing something well often comes from the appreciation of the hard work and effort it took to arrive at a level of expertise with it. I get a lot of personal satisfaction from working with Spanish-speaking families because I feel that I am being rewarded for the effort I put into learning Spanish since kindergarten. It's not just the effort over three decades. It's acknowledging the times I made a complete fool of myself inserting Portuguese for Spanish; the time I got lost at the border of Argentina, Paraguay, and Brazil while studying abroad in college because I didn't fully understand the directions given to me; or the countless times I have been met with looks that screamed, "I don't understand what you are saying!" If I'd lacked the grit and determination to keep going with Spanish, I would not be the gringo today who is actually complimented for his mastery of the language.

This is a personal example of grit—but it can be applied to countless situations children face as part of their development. Regardless of what path they choose, they need to become comfortable with investing themselves in their goals. This requires them to be able to address setbacks and other challenges, deal with unpleasant and uncomfortable situations, and not crumble in that moment because it is not going their way. Children also need to be comfortable with not seeing immediate results for their efforts and the distinct possibility that they will not initially succeed with their goals.

Many students are incredibly talented, which often means that they can get by without applying themselves. Eventually, though, their talent only carries them so far, and a complex problem arises that stumps them. Many such students are thus unequipped to deal with these stumbling blocks because they have never encountered a problem their talent couldn't solve. Regardless of the goal—earning admission to Harvard, becoming a doctor to find the cure for cancer, or creating the next Snapchat—today's kids need to be comfortable with a long journey filled with stumbling blocks along the way.

What distinguishes those geniuses and gifted people? Grit. While many people recognize Bill Gates as a transformative figure for the information age who dropped out of college to found Microsoft, fewer know of his earlier foray into tech entrepreneurship with Paul Allen: Traf-O-Data. Gates's first product failed. When it went to market, the device had multiple malfunctions and was a failure. Instead of giving up, the two founded Microsoft.

To horror enthusiasts, Stephen King is often the first legendary author who comes to mind. His own journey to success is as grueling as some of his stories are to read or watch. King's first novel was rejected by thirty publishers, and in frustration he threw it in the trash. His wife, Tabitha, picked it up and encouraged Stephen to finish it. He agreed, and the book known as *Carrie* came into existence. It was received with widespread acclaim. King has continued to write thrillers and mystery novels that have captured the imaginations of readers and moviegoers around the world.

What would have happened had these people lacked the grit to try again? The persistence and self-confidence that grit engenders in a person is what separates Gates and King from the countless other people who may be just as bright or talented but did not reach their own goals. University of Pennsylvania sociologist Angela Duckworth, who has studied grit for years, wrote in her book, *Grit*, that it is "the single trait in our complex and wavering nature that accounts for success." In a world with 5 percent acceptance rates to sought-after private and public universities and 1 percent hiring rates at industry-leading firms, it may also be the most important trait for children to develop to navigate the world and reach their goals.

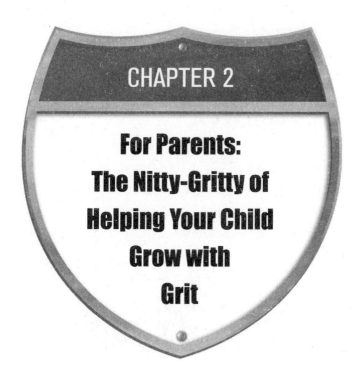

CHAPTER 2

For Parents: The Nitty-Gritty of Helping Your Child Grow with Grit

THERE IS NO RIGHT WAY TO HELP A CHILD develop grit for themselves. A general and simple rule to live by while fostering grit is: "Am I allowing them to grow in ways they need to for the long run?" If the answer is no, then we need to step back. Just like when a toddler who is learning to walk stumbles and starts to cry, we don't pick them up and carry them to where they are trying to go. Instead, the right thing to do is to encourage them to get back up and try again. It is okay to hold their hand, and eventually, they won't need help to walk confidently if they keep at it.

With older children facing more complex challenges, it is not as black-and-white, and parents often feel the stakes are much higher than they really are. Will that B on a final exam prevent students from getting into their top-choice college and ruin the rest of their life? No, and while we are on that subject, any college that has a de facto admission requirement to have straight As doesn't have a monopoly on that path to success in the first place (let's table that for a later part of the book).

So, helping a child develop grit requires parents to not ratchet up their advocacy skills and ability to wage World War III when the child receives an undesirable grade on an important project or test. While parents may know how to ask for feedback to learn how to improve or to advocate for themselves if an outcome is not just, children need to develop these traits themselves to be able to problem solve and grow into competent and independent adults. Give a child the space to learn from mistakes or areas for improvement. In addition, children need chances to advocate for themselves as these experiences also help a growing child become comfortable with coming up short. The humility that comes with acknowledging that there is room for improvement is critical for them to learn how to find fulfillment in their journey to success and prevent them from obsessing over the outcome.

DO: Let your child grow on their own.

A great example of this is how one of my clients helped encourage her son to use the college application process to learn how to better express himself through writing essays and interviewing. Christy was a former elementary school teacher, so maybe she had a leg up on the child development front. Either way, she recognized the college application process for what it is: a process that rewards applicants who are able to effectively describe their ability to add value to colleges.

Christy wanted her son to learn how to advocate for himself but wanted whatever he wrote to be true to who he was. Writing about ourselves is arguably one of the most awkward parts of the college application, and Ben, who was already painfully shy, had trouble expressing himself verbally or in writing. At our first meeting, I gave my usual spiel about the importance of essays and how they are a crucial part of the application process that really allows each student to show off their personality and creativity, something that isn't always reflected in grades or test scores. I told Christy that we would work with Ben to make his essays strong, even if personal writing wasn't his thing.

Christy stopped me right there. She made it very clear that beyond brainstorming ideas with him and working with him on grammar, neither I nor anyone else on my team would be allowed to touch his writing. "He should go to a school based on his words, not someone else's," she told me in a tone I imagined struck fear into the hearts of many a third grader back in her teaching days.

Of course, I obliged. Though we offered Ben advice and guidance at every meeting and helped him talk through his ideas, all the words on his college application were entirely his. In the end, he was rejected from his dream college—the University of California, Santa Barbara—which requires four essays as part of its application. Perhaps he would have been admitted had his essays been edited extensively to make the case more persuasively for admission. He ended up attending a less selective UC campus: UC Riverside.

Although it wasn't his first-choice school, it is the perfect fit for him. He is thriving academically, and the more relaxed social scene allowed him to come out of his shell. Had he not been encouraged to fight his own battles, he may have ended up at a college where he would have been overwhelmed from the get-go and prone to become a college dropout statistic.

Instead, Ben was given the gift of making life work himself and growing along the way. By instilling grit in him during the college application process, Christy taught Ben how to keep fighting even when things are tough. In the end, the outcome of his college application process was more rewarding because it was entirely his own, and it was hard-won.

DON'T: Fight your child's battles as a snowplow parent.

Like their namesake equipment, snowplow parents exist to remove obstacles because they mistakenly believe that this will lead to their child's long-term success. Unfortunately, they end up depriving their children of the ability to develop into resilient and independent adults, especially because they tend to be primarily focused on short-term accomplishments.

Deathly allergic to the idea of their children experiencing rejection or failure, snowplow parents can be found doing their children's homework, fighting every one of their battles (especially for extra points on exams), looking for loopholes to make life easier for their kids, or hiring others to prop their kids up to appear successful in the moment. They are, by force of habit and experience, well-versed in elementary school project design expectations and high school paper citation format.

I once counseled a parent named Chelsea, who had a Ph.D. in English literature from Columbia University. When it comes to college admissions, grades are important. In addition to test scores, grades are the first data point in the screening process: If applicants fail to meet an academic standard that each college decides on, they will automatically be rejected before admissions officers even open the file to read the essays. It's not a perfect system, but it's the only way admissions officers can even begin to sort through the increasing onslaught of applications they receive each year. The more academically rigorous the college is, the more stringent the cutoff point is for grades. Extremely selective schools like those in the Ivy League sometimes may only consider students with one B on their transcript, because the competition is too strong.

I knew this. Chelsea knew this too, and since she was bent on having her son continue her legacy at Columbia, she monitored his high school grades very closely—even more closely than her son did. It was as if she, and not her son, were the student. When he earned a B in his ninth-grade English class, she was distraught. Naturally, she called me.

On the phone, she began crying. Not knowing what else to do, I hastily repeated soothing phrases that I am accustomed to offering the "Ivy or bust" crowd about how admissions officers typically focus on the importance of an upward grade trend in high school. Once she finished crying, she began yelling because she felt her son's chances of going to an Ivy League college were over. (Clearly, I am bad at comforting people.)

I wanted to tell her something along the lines of "Chelsea, it's okay, it's not the end of the world. There are many fantastic colleges out there for your son! Even if he doesn't make it to the Ivy League, there are plenty of other colleges that offer incredible educations to prepare your son to reach his long-term goals."

But before I could say any of that, she screamed, "I have a Ph.D. in English literature from Columbia University, and I wrote his essays, and he still got a fucking B in the class!"

If I had thought I didn't know what to say when she was crying, I definitely didn't know what to say after that. I couldn't help but wonder: Was Chelsea angry because of her son's B, or because her own pride was wounded? But more importantly, how can we expect Chelsea's son to succeed in future English or writing assignments when he learned nothing from ninth grade because his mom did all his work? Beyond succeeding in English and writing, how can we expect him to succeed at life if, at the nascent age of fourteen, he already relies on his mom to do the hard work? How will he ever get anywhere in life without, well, grit?

Flash forward two years, and in the face of a rampant cheating problem, Chelsea's son's school switched from take-home writing assignments to timed in-class writing assignments. With no Chelsea to write for him, her son earned Bs in each of his English and history classes and effectively ended his chances of being admitted to the all-important Ivy League colleges his mom was so hell-bent on having him attend.

If we were to compare Chelsea's and Christy's sons, there might have been a point where Chelsea's son seemed like the one with the greater potential and brighter future, based on his artificially stellar high school performance and thanks to his mom's efforts. But learning from mistakes and how one can improve will propel Ben to succeed in the long term. Ben has grit, whereas Chelsea's son has a distraught mom and some As on early ninth-grade papers.

The scariest consequence of snowplow parenting is the dependence it creates for the child. Unable to develop the skills to advance in life independently, they rely on Mom, Dad, or whoever can plow the way for them to function.

Gail completed every single college application for her son, Derek. Derek (who, by the way, was a delight) refused to engage in the college process. Gail (also a delight) confided to me that she was getting her second college degree while completing all Derek's college papers and assignments.

Derek has come close to failing every exam he took in college. We (Gail, my team, and I) are still holding our breath to see if Derek will graduate. Gail had a minor panic attack when Derek considered switching to a computer science major because the classes would require him to use software that she knew nothing about. Worse, Derek is miserable because he is overwhelmed at college and still relies on his mother to fight his every battle as he is unable to advocate for himself.

As I'm watching the drama of Derek's life and Gail's possible second (or even third!) degree play out, I can't help wondering if Derek will grow up to be like Adam, one of my classmates from elementary school. Adam's mom, Carol, made fun of my third-grade geography report to my own mom's face.

In Carol's defense, eight-year-old me was barely able to write in a straight line. The title of my report dropped across my poster. My handwritten text was illegible (that part hasn't changed much with adulthood, unfortunately). However, in my defense, I did the entire report by myself, while Carol did Adam's entire project for him.

Carol, bless her heart, could not *believe* that my mom would let me turn in such a project. How could my mother stand idly by and watch this happen? Meanwhile, my mom was confused—was she supposed to sign off on everything I did in school? Or redo it? To a snowplow parent like Carol, the answer is a resounding yes. Which is why Adam's project resembled the work of an architect.

On school open house night, Adam's project was stowed away in a corner while my teacher, who was smart and probably saw right through Carol, prominently displayed my project in all its authentic, chicken-scratch glory in the center of the classroom. A snubbed Carol did not stay long at the open house. Seething with jealousy, she also avoided my mom for much of the school year.

But the open house didn't stop Carol. She went on to do many more of Adam's projects. When he did not qualify for high school honors classes based on tests he had to take himself, Carol decided to transfer him to another school, and we lost contact with them. According to Facebook, Carol went on to work for a prestigious university, presumably to ensure that her son would be admitted to it. It didn't seem to work. Now, some fifteen-plus years after we graduated from high school, Adam has yet to obtain a college degree and *still* lives at home. I imagine he now has plenty of time to learn how to do all his work on his own as an adult.

Adam, many of my peers, and today's students are sadly in good company. A *New York Times* article from 2019 provided shocking insight into how snowplow parenting has left millennials and Gen Zers incapable of dealing with the trials and tribulations of daily life.[7] Horror stories included one student who dropped out of college because there was a rat in the dorm room. If this child had known how to contact the housing office at their university, I imagine this challenge could have been resolved.

In one account detailing individual stories behind the skyrocketing college dropout rate, many college freshmen could not handle roommate disagreements, academic workload, and even cafeteria meal options. Coddled for their entire childhood, they couldn't socialize unless their parents set up playdates with their dorm neighbors or complained to employers when an internship didn't lead to a job.[8] Needless to say, if a student is promising enough to earn admission to Stanford but unable to make a plan to meet for coffee calls, the entire college admissions process should be called into question.

A recent poll designed to study the capabilities of the children of snowplow parents found that 76 percent of parents reminded their adult children of deadlines at school, 22 percent helped them study for college tests, 74 percent made appointments for them (including but not limited to doctor's appointments), and 15 percent of parents texted or called their children to wake them up every morning. Eleven percent of parents called to resolve their children's work issues, and 16 percent wrote a part of or all their children's job or internship applications. Fourteen percent made career decisions for their children, 12 percent gave more than $500 per month for rent or daily expenses, and 11 percent helped write an essay or school assignment.[9]

The problem has become pervasive for employers too. In a survey by Michigan State University, a quarter of employers reported receiving calls or e-mails from parents urging them to hire their child, and some parents even showed up for their child's job interview.[10]

While there is nothing wrong with reminding an adult child to study, being a sounding board for a career, or coordinating appointments for a dependent on a parent's insurance plan, parents weaken their child's ability to stand independently on their own two feet when they act as a human alarm clock or submit job applications on behalf of their kids. Even if we think it is better to do the damn job application to get them out of the proverbial basement, at what point does a parent think it is in their child's best interest for the parent to resolve a work issue for them? How will this adult child ever get promoted if their boss knows the parent is involved in their career or doing their work for them?

DO: Embrace their journey by prioritizing your child's growth over short-term wins.

In my community, there is a public high school known as one of the most academically rigorous public high schools in the country. I worked with a student, Sara, who attended that school and studied for hours every day. Her grades were impressive, but she did earn a few Bs in college-level math and science courses. This meant that her transcript was not strong enough to be admitted to the most selective colleges in the nation like MIT or Stanford. But because she took tough classes with peers who provided stiff competition, she truly gained the skills needed to study engineering, her passion. Her hard work also meant that taking the SAT was a relative breeze for her. The rigor from her high school coursework prepared her for the exam, and she scored in the top 1 percent of global test takers.

In the end, Sara studied engineering at the University of Southern California. While not a school that pops to mind like MIT or Caltech when we think of engineering, it nonetheless has a strong engineering program. Sara earned fantastic grades in college and reported that while the work was challenging, it was the same level of challenge as her high school coursework. Because she put in the work, she was prepared for a bigger stage to seize the opportunities she had. She took advantage of the extensive Trojan network throughout Southern California and pursued internships at aerospace companies. She will graduate with a résumé defined by skills and experiences that will make her able to immediately add value to any employer's organization.

Meanwhile, I was also working with Laurie, a mom whose son was in Sara's grade. They attended middle school together, but come ninth grade, while Sara moved on to the local public high school,

Laurie decided that the academic rigor would be too much for her son to handle, and she didn't want him to risk getting bad grades and suffering the consequences during the college application process. She decided to enroll him in an easy private high school that offered classes like Honors Art. His class schedule was filled with fluff honors classes, and he boasted an impressive 4.8 (out of 4.0) GPA by his junior year.

Laurie was ecstatic. She was sure he would be a strong candidate for Stanford, his dream school. But his curriculum was watered down, and the lack of rigor meant he wasn't learning important concepts he needed.

And it showed. When it came time to take the SAT college entrance exam, his test score was in the 40th percentile for the state and would not even make him eligible for the lowly state school fifteen minutes away.

Laurie, unwilling to face the facts and maybe try to help her son improve his study habits, began to rail against how the system was biased and she would prefer if her son applied to colleges and universities that adopted a more holistic approach to evaluating candidates. I didn't know if she meant that she wanted me to find her kid an Ivy League university that would weigh an honors photography class on the same level as a skills-based college entrance exam, or something else. At the end of the day, Laurie's son was rejected from every highly competitive college he applied to. He enrolled in a state university that made admissions decisions purely based on his GPA without looking at the rigor of courses, his test scores, or his essays.

Trying to game the system may allow for early victories for a child but leave them woefully unprepared for long-term success and fulfillment. As I tell all students we work with in the first meeting,

I am more concerned about where they will be in life in ten years rather than where they will enroll in college. When it comes to preparing children for their futures, it is important to cast the near term as a means to an end and not a shortsighted obsession for bragging rights. While we don't need to make life any more difficult than it already is, we don't need to make it so easy that kids are unprepared for real life. A college education is a means to an end, not the be-all and end-all. The grit and tenacity they develop as part of their education will prepare them for the struggles they will face to reach their long-term goals and full potential.

DON'T: Use excuses to justify shortcomings or shield them from adversity.

Children are going to fail sometimes. It's inevitable while they are young and learning. However, rather than encouraging them to embrace and learn from the setback, many snowplow parents try to justify their children's shortcomings and failures by blaming them on external circumstances. This creates a victim culture for children to explain away everything. Like a revisionist history, this type of snowplower deprives their children of the chance to learn from past experiences out of fear they will hurt their child's fragile ego or, even more importantly, their own fragile ego as it relates to what their child can accomplish.

This form of snowplowing is more commonly deployed when the parent is unable to remove the obstacles from their child's path ahead of time. I worked with a high schooler, Rachel, who was a good, but not great, student. Rachel did what was asked of her but did not go above and beyond when it came to her schoolwork, activities, or involvement in the community. Rachel had realistic expectations for where she wanted to apply to college based on her grades and résumé.

Her mom, however, had grand visions of Rachel attending the hyperselective "Ivy equivalents" that have 5 percent acceptance rates and admissions practices similar to the Ivies. And as most teenagers know, when Mom and Dad's vision conflicts with your vision, Mom and Dad's vision is probably going to win.

There was just one problem for this snowplow parent: Rachel's ACT college entrance exam. At Vanderbilt, Rachel's mom's dream school for her child, the incoming class ACT average was between 33 and 35 out of 36. Yes, that meant admitted students had close to perfect scores and were in the top 1 percent of global test takers. At most colleges following the pandemic, the SAT and ACT have become optional. However, according to information submitted to the U.S. Department of Education regarding their admissions and enrollment statistics, up to 75 percent of students that were admitted to selective colleges that accept the SAT or ACT submitted them.[11] In plain English, competitive applicants are expected to submit an SAT or ACT score. Some applicants may be excused from the testing requirement due to financial hardships or other circumstances that prevent them from studying for the test, but in general, applicants to selective schools should aim to submit a test score that is in line with that school's score range.

Rachel's test score was a problem. At 24, Rachel's score was over 10 points lower than the range required for Vanderbilt. While the score was okay (top 26 percent of global test takers), it wasn't strong enough for Vanderbilt. And her mom knew it.

As soon as the scores came out, Rachel's mom began to make excuses for her child. Among her excuses were the following:

- She and Rachel's dad were getting divorced during Rachel's ACT exam, so it was a bad time.
- Thanks to the pandemic, Rachel's education was not the same as the education she would have gotten in a classroom. (Never mind that all the other ACT test takers had also been negatively impacted by the pandemic.)
- Last, but not least, Rachel couldn't breathe because she was wearing a mask during the exam. Thus, the process was prejudiced against her daughter. Rachel was a victim of the process. She would contact Vanderbilt and inform them of this injustice immediately. ("I'm glad Rachel doesn't want to be a surgeon who has to wear a mask for hours in surgery!" I joked. The joke, needless to say, did not go over well.)

While Rachel's mom was attempting to explain away her unqualified ACT scores, she was actually suggesting to me that her daughter's shortcomings were not her fault, and that even though Rachel didn't meet the standards, it was out of her control. Conversely, this logic would also mean that anything Rachel did well was also governed by forces outside her control. By creating excuses, she transformed the child from an active participant and manager of her own life to a passive observer.

When snowplow parents take action on their excuses, they impact their child's entire life. One of my students, Dana, was admitted to her dream college but, as many people do in the initial transition to college, struggled to make friends. The school offered everything Dana was looking for in the ideal college experience: the specialized academic program she wanted to study, access to nature and hikes that she enjoyed, and the most important part of all—a mountain biking club.

Dana joined a sorority, a mountain biking club, and the winter sports team, and it seemed as though she had surrounded herself with people with similar interests. But Dana was shy and struggled to connect with her peers. Even though this may seem like a common problem, Dana lacked the skills to make friends, and it wasn't just because she was shy. Even in high school, her mom had been in charge of making playdates for her so she would have friends to hang out with.

Her mom, who probably couldn't make playdates for her college-age daughter who was now a thousand miles away, did what she could. She made an appointment with me, sat down, and made excuses. Too many people at Dana's university identified with "they/them" pronouns, and as a result, the school wasn't welcoming to cisgender heterosexual students like Dana. Dana's mom was devastated by the "liberal agenda" at the university and that Dana wasn't able to find friends as a result. I wondered what percentage of the student body actually identified as nonbinary or transgender and how many tens of thousands of the 40,000-plus students at the university would conform to Dana's mom's standard of normalcy and be suitable friend candidates for her daughter. Surely she could find three or four people to hang out with irrespective of whatever liberal agenda her mom railed against.

Rather than guiding her daughter to own and be comfortable with the hardships of starting over socially and encouraging her to put herself out there to make friends and be patient if things didn't work out right away, Dana's mom wanted to blame her child's unhappiness on something else.

A few days later, I received a call from Dana's mom, who told me she wanted to transfer her daughter to a college in a red state where people didn't lead introductions with their pronouns and would need my team's help with the transfer application process. After all, Dana couldn't be expected to fit in with *those* kinds of people.

So she hijacked Dana's life as she did with her social calendar while she lived under the same roof and insisted that her daughter apply to a large public university in a different state. The irony wasn't lost on me that Dana's mom's new dream school was located in a liberal enclave that prides itself on its inclusivity and rainbow flags are hoisted in countless windows in buildings around campus. I'm rooting for Dana in the new school but not holding my breath because, apparently, all it takes is one person who prefers to refer to themselves as "they" to prevent this snowplowed child from making any friends with other people.

DO: Teach your child the right way to persevere.

We live in an era when an obsession with outcomes leads many young people to think that the results are more important than the growth journey. Instant gratification and stories of overnight successes like college dropouts Mark Zuckerberg and Evan Spiegel becoming impactful tech entrepreneurs and billionaires relatively quickly are the fantasies for many aspiring computer programmers. Influencers like the Kardashian and Jenner clan make it seem easy to become fabulously wealthy and lead lives that seem too good to be true. This makes many impressionable young people wonder, *Is the hard work worth it? Is there some better, easier, quicker way to get me to my goals?*

But for every Zuckerberg or Spiegel, there are people who fell from grace. Sam Bankman-Fried and Elizabeth Holmes, founders of crypto platform FTX and medical diagnosis testing startup Theranos, respectively, were initially praised as revolutionaries for their overnight successes in their respective industries, only to be exposed as frauds. To go from gracing the covers of magazines and hobnobbing with senators and industry titans to facing decades behind bars is a steep fall from grace.

When speaking with students whose perspective is framed by social media and moments captured to display to the world, it often feels that the fall is sometimes a footnote in those people's stories. The truth is, the fall is their legacy and what will define the rest of their lives. Even shows like *Narcos* and *Money Heist* make audiences root for the bad guys.

Now, by no means am I suggesting that our culture promotes or rewards criminal or immoral conduct. It just requires parents to hold themselves and their children to the highest standards to ensure that their children learn how to succeed the right way: on their terms, in a sustainable and impactful way.

Success needs to be sustainable for it to be fulfilling. I've had students admit to me that they felt immense pressure to cheat on an exam to maintain their A in a class. Rather than judge them—they know what they did was wrong—I pose one simple question: How are they going to be prepared for the next test if they don't build a foundation with the current material? There are no shortcuts in this world, and sooner or later, anything that seems like one is bound to be a dead end from which it is much harder to recover.

Cheating has become pervasive in high school. Sixty-four percent of students admitted to cheating on a test, 58 percent admitted to plagiarism, and 95 percent said they participated in some form of cheating, whether it was on a test, plagiarism, or copying homework.[12]

Yet cheating flies in the face of grit. If we define grit as the ability to delay gratification to reach a long-term goal, it means we must teach children to forsake short-term gains that may prevent us from obtaining long-term success by enduring obstacles and challenges that will prepare us for the journey ahead. Cheating means not acquiring the skills, concepts, and perspectives needed to sustain ourselves every step of the way.

Rather than prioritizing straight As on a report card, parents can approach each semester as a chance to learn the key concepts from those classes needed to advance to the next level and reach one's long-term goals. Rather than encouraging kids to cheat on the court or the field, parents should encourage their student-athletes to develop the skills they need to grow and play at a higher level. When it comes to athletic recruitment, coaches do not just look at a player's stats. They watch how a player plays and make a recruitment decision based on their ability to contribute to their team. Parents need to explain this to their children in no uncertain terms.

The pervasiveness of cheating and an obsession with keeping up with everyone else in a competitive environment can influence any well-behaved kid who is facing intense pressure to perform at home or in their communities. In my experience, cheating is most rampant in the highest-achieving school communities. No one wants to be left behind, but I cannot help but wonder if a culture that rewards outcomes rather than the growth journey is partially to blame for the rise in young people incapable of managing their lives as adults.

I worked with a family whose son Kyle was diagnosed with ADHD at a young age. As a result of his diagnosis, he received accommodations during elementary school for extended time on tests. With much work and a family focus, he was able to manage his learning difference with incredible success. While he did rely on medication, Kyle grew into a strong student who performed well on tests in high school. As he progressed throughout high school, Kyle was offered the chance to receive extended time on high school exams to accommodate his ADHD. Kyle, however, declined as he did not need accommodations to finish the exams and do well on them.

When sophomore year rolled around, Kyle took a diagnostic ACT exam and did relatively poorly on it. The tight timing on the test did not play to his strengths, and he scheduled a meeting with his mom and me. Kyle wanted to request extended time on the ACT as he had heard of multiple students at his über-competitive high school acquiring learning difference diagnoses from pay-to-play educational psychologists to get extra time on the ACT.

Time is the biggest lever on the ACT, and studies have shown that having extended time can make a world of difference as the short amount of time per question is partially what makes the test challenging.

I don't know if Kyle thought it was the right time to introduce this idea to his mom at our meeting or not, but Tracey was blindsided by the request and immediately made her displeasure with the idea known to her son.

"Kyle, you have never used extended time in high school before, and now when it's convenient to you, you want to all of a sudden ask for it?" she asked in an exasperated tone.

Kyle, focused on the short-term gain and feeling the peer pressure to keep up with his classmates, responded, "Mom, everyone is getting it at school. It's helping them get perfect scores on the test, which is what I need to go to an Ivy."

Tracey was not impressed. "What gives? You need to learn how to take this test. These accommodations are for people who need them to level up the playing field. You are a straight-A student. You have to work harder than them, but that is what makes you so successful. You can do this. You have done this your whole life. We are not going to change course now. And if you can't get the score you need on this test to go to the college you want, then it wasn't meant to be."

There was nothing more I needed to or could have added to this. Tracey handled this brilliantly and reminded her son that he was the keeper of his own destiny. He would not look for a shortcut to game the system like the numerous parents who were convicted of cheating in the Varsity Blues college admissions scandal. Tracey managed to teach her son grit in this exchange. He would be responsible for his success and would have to work hard for it—which is what he needed then, now, and in the future much more than a strong ACT score.

Kyle had to study long hours for the ACT. Whereas his peers went off to play sports or hang out after their ACT tutoring sessions, Kyle had to study on his own in addition to his tutoring sessions just to keep up with his peers. Every Saturday for weeks, he sat himself down in his bedroom to take a self-timed practice test. He ended up scoring a 33 on the ACT, which put him in the top 1 percent of global test takers, and I was proud of him. But more importantly than scoring well on the exam, I believe this experience prepared him for college and his ultimate goal of becoming a doctor, which will require him to take challenging tests for the next fifteen years of his life.

I have worked with several of Kyle's close friends who late in their high school education started complaining about how they were running out of time on school exams. This seemed to be a play to get extended time on the ACT to boost their score, and they ultimately used accommodations to do well on the test. I know that they lack the grit needed to overcome each obstacle they will also face on their path to becoming doctors. Regardless of where Kyle was admitted to college, the sacrifices he made to study for the test will empower him to reach his goals. His peers have not learned this critical life lesson and instead have been rewarded for finding a shortcut. Sooner or later, they will reach a dead end that cannot be overcome. And because that experience will happen later in life, it will be more painful to learn.

DON'T: Scorch the earth as a terminator parent for your child to win at all costs.

The Varsity Blues scandal, which resulted in dozens of affluent parents going to prison and their unqualified progeny being unceremoniously expelled from many of the nation's most selective colleges, taught us that a win-at-all-costs mentality is a road to nowhere. While there are likely many others out there who will lie, cheat, and steal to get to where they need to be or want their children to go who may never get caught for their rule-breaking behavior, it shows that it is not worth the risk to engage in behavior that may achieve short-term gains for the child that harms them in the long run.

I refer to this type of parenting as *terminator parenting*. No matter the potential for harm, the win-at-all-costs mentality truly has the potential to destroy the child's perception of what is right and future avenues for growth. Scorched-earth terminators are known for threatening to sue their kids' schools (and sometimes carrying out their threats) when they get Bs for final grades on the basis that the teacher's grading was unfair. They do the same when their child doesn't make the varsity sports team, alleging biases or unequal treatment under the law. They move schools midyear when they disagree with what their children are reading in English class. They withhold charitable gifts to their kids' schools and band together with other terminator parents to exert influence on the schools' policies to benefit their children. These parents pay tutors to take their kids' exams for them. The list goes on.

Along the way, terminator parents normalize this type of behavior for their children and inhibit them from growing in ways they need to actually be prepared for the opportunities their parents crave for them. But this type of behavior has a funny and poetic way of catching up with the students.

Most families who work with me share their kids' college essays for feedback to improve them. Tina, however, was fiercely guarded with her daughter's essays. I was shocked when her daughter was admitted and received an early notification to UCLA well before the overwhelming majority of admitted applicants found out. Her admission decision came out the day that students with physical disabilities were admitted so that they could secure accessible housing. I was perplexed as they never disclosed any disabilities to me over the many years we worked together, but based on their behavior, I suspected—along with many who knew them well—that they lied about a disability as part of their application to earn admission to a school that the student was probably not qualified to attend.

Fast-forward a few months later, and her daughter was assigned to a dorm for students with disabilities, and the mother raged to all who would listen that her daughter was struggling to meet "normal" people because of her "accidental" dorm placement.

But the point of the story lies with her further continuation of the story. Rather than recognizing the fact that there would be consequences for cutting corners in this process and life when the daughter was not admitted to a single sorority on campus, Tina reached out to ask for my help to sue the school's sorority system for discrimination. She would not explain what the basis of her lawsuit would be beyond "unfair treatment." She couldn't seem to make up her mind as to whether her daughter had a disability that required accommodation or belonged in a "normal" dormitory with other students who did not require accommodation.

The irony wasn't lost on me that now this mom sought to wrap herself in the argument used to ensure that students with disabilities are entitled to accommodations on campus to receive an equal and fair education alongside the rest of their peers. This same parent moved her younger child who was getting Bs at the public high school to a private high school on the other side of town. She will stop at nothing to get her children what they want in the moment. Rather than teaching them what grit is and how to develop it, she has raised kids who complain incessantly about factors outside their control and embrace the victim card at any chance they can. As a result, over a dozen sororities declined to accept this student into their organizations. Perhaps an entire school community saw through the games and the complaining? This student now speaks of transferring to another school. It seems like all the scorched earth led to nowhere rather than the journey to happiness that may have been achieved with grit.

The irony of it all is that most of these bad behaviors aren't conducted by bad people. As irrational and crazy as these parent examples may seem, all of them are caring parents who just want to see their children succeed. Desperation drives them to create shortcuts to lighten the load for their kids. (Let's face it, no one wants to see their kid struggle.) But grit, though uncomfortable to gain, is an invaluable skill. Students who possess grit will be able to forge a happier and more successful life than those who took shortcuts. As uncomfortable as it is, it is a parental duty to guide their children through long hours of hard work and appreciate their efforts, so that they can achieve their dreams and be fulfilled by them. This way, parents, in turn, can also achieve their dreams for their children: seeing them successful and happy.

CHAPTER 3

For Students: Gritting Your Teeth and Getting Out of Your Sweats: What a Young Person Should Do to Develop Grit

WHILE PARENTS MUST START AND GUIDE their children on the path to health, happiness, and financial independence, at a certain point, their children will take the reins and assume ownership of their lives. Some of these key milestones can occur while they are still young and living at home. As a refresher, the three key traits that admissions officers look for in college applications are grit, leadership, and passion. For students interested in maximizing outcomes in this process and preparing themselves for life beyond college, it behooves them to develop these traits.

Passion and leadership seem easier to measure. To develop and demonstrate passion, a student interested in healthcare fields can volunteer or intern at a hospital. Students interested in engineering can join their school's robotics team and see if they enjoy building autonomous robots while signaling to admissions officers that they are dedicating themselves to their passions. Leadership can also be developed by serving on the student council or as a leader in a variety of capacities like club officers or team captains.

Grit sometimes lies below the surface and develops in ways unique to an individual. How can we tell if someone has grit? Surely, someone who has overcome hardship. But not everyone has these trying experiences to endure, which is okay. If a student has never faced a life experience that required grit, they should consider themselves blessed.

Most students and their parents turn to sports as a natural source of grit. At a personal level, I believe sports do instill grit in participants. Becoming skilled at a sport requires dedication and commitment. All but a small handful of student-athletes will grow comfortable with not winning every game, match, or event. But we have moved past the world where all young people are expected to participate in sports inside or outside school.

In the college admissions process, grit is defined as the ability to overcome life's day-to-day challenges. An excellent way an applicant can demonstrate acquired grit is by handling a part-time job. For millennials, who never achieved financial independence, and Gen Zers, infamous for relying on Mom and Dad to do everything for them, the one thing parents can't do is diffuse the next world war because their kids put the wrong type of milk in a latte.

DO: Get a part-time job.

A part-time job where a young person is the low person on the totem pole is one of the best ways to prepare for the challenges that await in the real world. Need to learn how to deal with difficult people who are impossible to please? There is probably no better place than *any* service business today to become well-versed in difficult customers and how to address a never-ending list of problems that may or may not exist. Want to learn how to manage a difficult boss? Working for a manager who doesn't care if you want to go to medical school or become a computer programmer in the future is a great reminder that the world doesn't revolve around any of us when we need to flip a burger or bag groceries. Do you know how to ensure that the team delivers on its expectations? Covering for an apathetic or absentee coworker teaches you how to be accountable to make sure the job gets done. To top it off, many service workers make fifteen to twenty dollars per hour now.

My practice is located in one of the most affluent parts of the United States, and I once had a parent tell me that his daughter doesn't need to work. Objectively, he is 100 percent right. She will likely never need to either. But that precisely underscores why that child needs to work more than most: to learn critical life skills that are needed to deal with uncomfortable times that are easy to be shielded from when occupying positions of privilege.

It does not matter what type of job you have. It can be in food service, retail, or hospitality. You can babysit or tutor. You just need to be held accountable and learn what it is like to solve other people's problems as your job.

There is an added bonus—in an era when student dropout rates are skyrocketing—because admissions officers prioritize life experiences that prepare applicants for college and beyond. An aspiring Harvard student may think McDonald's is beneath them, but cleaning the kitchen or bathrooms will prepare them for dealing with uncomfortable moments in college.

I once worked with a student, Clarissa, who told me that while she was working one summer at a tutoring center, she had to deal with parents who would scream at her in Chinese. Since she was the only Mandarin-speaking employee, her boss asked her to deal with them while still being professional and polite. She informed me that even though it was a bad experience, she was grateful because she had learned how to deal with difficult people and not get flustered even when they are being unreasonable or downright rude. This student was primed to write a college essay that asked about her greatest strength or talent.

Rather than writing an essay about her ability to solve complex chemistry problems or score game-winning goals and boast about experiences that countless other high achievers could discuss in their college essays, Clarissa decided to take a more humble brag approach. To signal to college admissions officers that she possesses grit, she told about the life skills she had acquired through her talent of maintaining her composure in difficult situations. It helped her earn admission to UCLA, which is the most applied-to public university in the country, with 150,000 applicants vying for 5,000 spots.

It's not just about college admission. At a personal level, Clarissa learned the art of talking on the phone, a skill that many people her age struggle to do. For many young people who came of age in an era of instant messaging through text, a phone call without warning is an act of aggression. Phone anxiety is so severe and pervasive among many younger workers that some large employers have resorted to hiring coaches who charge up to $500 an hour to coach employees so that they can communicate over the phone without fear.

Working a part-time, entry-level job also helps with the most sought-after career paths. The summer before my senior year of college, I landed a coveted Wall Street investment banking summer internship. The summer analyst who sat at the desk next to mine, Matt, was brilliant. In my opinion, he was the smartest intern in the entire class of thirty. He studied finance and computer science at MIT. He could lap me in making sophisticated financial models and was probably better at the job than many full-time employees with several years of experience.

Matt had just one problem: his attitude. This was Matt's first job, and he didn't know what it meant to be the grunt on the team. Matt had grown up in Aspen, and he seemed to think the world revolved around him and his brilliance. He had never had a part-time job doing anything, as his dad was a very successful attorney. Not once did he ask our group's administrative assistant if she needed any help putting together pitch books. Nor did he ever offer to grab coffee for anyone stuck on a long conference call. In short, he didn't know how to read the situation and help others in ways that would make the team not just appreciate his work skills but like working with him.

At the end of the internship, each group could choose to make an offer to their summer analysts for a full-time position when they graduated the following year. Matt couldn't help mocking my technical skills and suggesting that I would never be hired for the position. But all summer long, relying on my experience babysitting and tutoring in high school, and later working part-time during my college semesters, I found ways to help everyone on the team in a manner that brought me closer to them. My two most pleasant surprises on the final day of the internship: (1) being offered a full-time position and (2) finding out that Matt did not get that offer. In my exit interview, my boss told me that they "could teach me how to be a banker, but they can't teach someone how to be a team player."

DON'T: Worry about the other F-word (failure).

In an era when parents go on TikTok to post not only game-winning goals and shots but also college acceptance reaction videos, it may seem like this world has evolved into a black-and-white framework that presents you with two outcomes in life: You win or you lose. This could not be further from the truth.

Yes, some events have clear outcomes. In sports, a person or team is almost always crowned the winner. The opposing side is therefore the loser. Yes, with college admissions, some are awarded a coveted spot at a selective university; many more are not. Some may be hired for their dream job while thousands of other applicants come up just short. But beyond this narrow set of examples, there are no true, realized losses for any of us to endure. Each "close, but no cigar" moment is a chance for a person—young, old, somewhere in between—to learn, grow, and prepare for the next chance to achieve their goals.

All of us need to adopt a growth mindset that is free of fear of the other F-word: failure. In life, every experience is a chance to grow and learn. Even if we are not successful, we can understand how to improve or modify our approach to reach a more favorable outcome in the future.

While we can feel the weight of the world on our shoulders during a penalty kick to try to win a soccer game or when we open the first page of an ACT test booklet on exam day, if the shot is errant or our mind goes blank, the only question we need to ask ourselves is, *What can I do differently the next time?* And there will always be a next time when we can improve just a little bit to reach our goals.

When I meet students for the first time, I tell them, "To be successful in this process just requires you to give it your best shot." I never say to any student that they "need to be the best" to reach their goals. The college admissions process, and life in general, is a growth process, measuring and rewarding applicants who commit themselves to grow as much as they can. Every advanced class, extracurricular activity, and new experience is a chance for students to learn new concepts, develop new skills, and find their path in life. Even if they come up short with the immediate goal of getting into a particular college or earning an award, they are still moving closer to making the most of their lives.

With this mindset, none of us can fail in life. As long as we pick ourselves up along the way, we come closer to succeeding in the long term with what we are meant to do.

One of the best examples of this I can provide is from a student, Chris, whom I grew rather close to over the years. I met Chris at the tail end of his sophomore year of high school. Chris took the most challenging classes at his high school and initially did so because he thought it would help him get into a more selective college. Chris did not earn straight As in these classes and was pretty devastated when I met him and explained how that would pan out in the college admissions process. I thought I may have scared him off after discussing this with him, but he came back and informed me that he appreciated that he was being pushed to learn more and write more effectively in his advanced history and English classes.

Chris also tried his utmost outside the classroom. He worked hard to make his school's cross-country team but was typically found at the back of the pack in races. And he was passed over despite his efforts to be the editor of his school's newspaper.

Battle-tested and scarred, Chris kept at it. With every B on his transcript and every lackluster race, Chris grew more comfortable in his own skin and the fact that he would have to try hard in life and not always initially succeed with his efforts. But he kept at it. He developed the confidence to put himself out there, which allowed him to take his best shot and apply for a summer research internship at the University of California, San Diego. He was accepted.

Even though Chris wasn't admitted to his top-choice university, he earned a scholarship to attend Tulane, where he has now become an assistant editor at the college newspaper and is excelling at opportunities that he came up short with in high school. Had Chris not tried and failed in high school at his many ambitious goals, he would likely not have been prepared to make the most of his college experience. If anything, Chris didn't fail, even in high school. Instead, he gained the skills and perspective he needed for a larger stage that was a better fit for him.

It is hard to tune out the negativity and the keeping-up-with-the-Joneses mentality upon which social media is built. Each of us will be happier and more productive if we run our own race and worry less about what others are doing. With each stumble, we need not compare ourselves to those who reached our goals before us. We will get there if we allow ourselves the time and kindness we ultimately need to reach our goals.

Reject the artificial and false choice that everything in life is a competition. We thrive where we are meant to do so—and on our own schedule—if we invest the time and energy in ourselves and our goals. Yes, along the way, someone else may make a varsity sports team that we don't make. Someone else may win the student council race, and someone else may be admitted to our dream school while we are rejected, but that is okay. None of those steps are critical to us ultimately becoming the people we are meant to be. We are going to fail in life, but as long as we keep at it, we will have more successes than failures overall, because our failures will inform our successes. The goal in life is not to be perfect; it's to learn and grow.

So let's get very comfortable with the other F-word, because each failure we experience brings us closer to when we actually say that we've succeeded.

DO: Embrace the journey by building skills.

Life is a collection of twists and turns. We will all be rewarded for embracing the journey and acknowledging that we are the keepers of our own destiny. Each of us will be rewarded for our grit to reach our goals.

When we are young, many of us like to map out what our lives will look like. Our parents may try to plan it out for us too. Go to [insert name brand of college], become [insert high-prestige career], save up to buy a house, marry, have children, and then start the process over for your children.

Sounds simple, right? Real life couldn't be further from this fantasy. Real life is unpredictable and can be messy, which is what makes it so interesting and rewarding when we finally achieve what fulfills each of us as individuals.

To be happy we need to embrace a part of the journey that at times can be incredibly uncomfortable: Our ultimate destinations are unknown. If anyone would have told me twenty years ago in my sophomore English class that I would be writing this book and working with kids, I would have said they were nuts. Back then,

I thought I wanted to be a lawyer. Along the way, I did become a lawyer. I hated every moment of it and was so grateful that I discovered what inspired me and make me tick. It was a complete 180, but had I not had faith in myself and that I would be okay regardless of not knowing where I was headed, I wouldn't have settled into what brings me joy.

Rather than trying to make ourselves fit into boxes that aren't appropriate for who we truly are or modifying our behavior to please others, including our parents, we need to stay true to ourselves and equip ourselves with the skills and perspective we need to reach goals in the future that are still to be determined.

The careers that parents encourage their kids to pursue today may no longer exist in the future. The most promising future fields that will be relevant when you are on the cusp of becoming an independent adult may still be waiting to be created. Keep an open mind, and rather than focus solely on specific goals, commit yourself to developing skills and perspectives that prepare you for a still-undefined future. Regardless of what you end up becoming, you can start today to improve the analytical, leadership, and communication skills that will serve you in a variety of fields. Becoming fluent in a language like Spanish will help regardless of whether you work in health care or as an engineer. Said differently, focus on tangible and concrete skills rather than rigid steps for goals that may no longer apply or be available to you.

Back to my own example: While law school and the practice of law weren't for me, I appreciate that they shaped my mind and taught me how to write and advocate more effectively. Had I not gone to law school, I don't think I would be as successful as a college admissions adviser. Without the moment when I was truly miserable and forced to ask myself what I wanted to do with my life, I wouldn't have landed on what I chose to do and become. Now, years after going to (and suffering through) law school, I am grateful that I went. It helped make me the person I am now.

The same is true for a student I worked with named Layla. Layla is an only child who had a lot of pressure to do well in school and become successful to take after her high-achieving parents. Layla hit a few rough patches in high school and earned Cs in key classes her junior year. She was captain of her high school's cheerleading team and was deeply involved in meaningful service activities. She did very well on her ACT. Still, when the time came to apply to college, I had to break the difficult news: Harvard and UCLA, her family's initial goals, would be tough to achieve. At the time, Layla wanted to be a lawyer and part of the reason they came to work with me was their concern that Layla should go to a prestigious undergraduate school to help her become a distinguished attorney.

Nothing could be further from the truth. The legal profession is more concerned about where lawyers attend law school rather than where they received their undergraduate degrees. After I explained that to her parents, their concern turned to Layla's odds of earning admission to a prominent law school if she did not attend a prestigious undergraduate institution. Also not true, as I explained that selective law schools cannot give a boost to applicants applying from prestigious colleges. Like with college admissions, graduate schools evaluate applicants based on how well they do within their school communities.

So, with her nerves assuaged, Layla applied to many colleges. Yes, she applied to UCLA and Harvard. And despite her best efforts, Layla was rejected from both those universities. But Layla was admitted to her backup choice, the University of Arizona, with a *full-tuition scholarship.* Layla was concerned about what people would think, as some in our community viewed it as a party school. I explained to her that she did not need to worry about what people in our community thought. She would just need to stay focused on herself and her goals and do the best she could. More importantly, with the hundreds of thousands of dollars her parents would be saving by not paying for her undergrad education, she would be able to go to law school without the crushing student loans that most lawyers struggle to repay.

Layla enrolled at Arizona, a school that was not on her radar throughout high school. She had a blast in college. She joined a sorority and became the president. She became a certified fitness instructor and taught classes at the gym to other students and members of the community. Just as importantly, she discovered that she didn't want to be a lawyer. Rather than pursuing law, Layla decided that she wanted to become a certified public accountant (CPA) because she enjoyed the detective work and math required to tie out companies' and individuals' finances.

Along the way, she earned close to perfect grades and applied to the top graduate-level accounting programs in California during her senior year of college. Layla was admitted to all of them and ultimately enrolled at the University of California, Irvine, with *another* full scholarship. Layla will graduate in a few years with no student loans for her entire education. She found her path because she made the most of every opportunity that she had. She kept an open mind and was true to who she was rather than the idea of who she or her parents wanted her to be. In my opinion, Layla's journey is one of the most promising and successful ones I have seen and not because her education was free. Rather, she embraced the journey to become the person who she is now: on her journey to health, happiness, and financial independence.

Grit, by definition, is not something any of us enjoy developing. But the journey to obtain it for ourselves prepares us to face challenges head-on and overcome them. Grit makes us resilient. To acquire grit, each of us is tested—and once we possess it, we will continue to be tested again and again. The process of ingraining grit allows us to see how strong we are, and that is as invaluable as grit itself.

FINAL THOUGHTS ON GRIT

WE NEED TO HELP YOUNG PEOPLE on their path to adulthood become comfortable with what makes them uncomfortable, especially when it's failure. Children actually experience few if any permanent failures. Rejected from Harvard for undergrad? That is okay; 99 percent of other applicants were also rejected there. But that doesn't mean that Harvard is forever out of the picture if that is the true goal. There is always the chance to apply there for grad school for a program that is probably more tailored to one's passions. Rather than place blame on the process, the system, or some teacher who is holding students accountable for their progress in the classroom, we can focus on being accountable for what is within our control and look to make the most of every situation we encounter. Not all of them will be positive, but that is precisely what makes each victory we achieve so meaningful.

Kids are more resilient than we sometimes acknowledge. We just need to give them the chance to develop their grit as much as possible. While life can be trying, we do them no favors in shielding them from reality. Some of the most monumental figures in history gained the grit they needed by dealing with setbacks early in life. We should study those experiences closely and ask what contributed to their success. We can encourage kids to look to them as role models rather than the naturally gifted who excel initially due to luck or circumstance. While the accomplishments of the lucky may be impressive, perhaps we need to be more mindful of upholding and respecting those who achieved things in life in ways similar to how our children will be expected to grow in the future.

I believe that snowplowing comes from a good place: a parent's desire for their child to succeed. However, with snowplowing we go to extremes and set children up to fail rather than succeed in the long term. By focusing on short-term victories, we lose sight of the big picture and our commitment to ensuring that children develop the skills and perspective they need to grow into healthy, happy, and financially independent adults.

Rather than look for loopholes or ways to guarantee children earn As on every book report and assignment, parents should encourage kids to approach assignments as opportunities to develop skills. Rather than focusing on kids earning admission to a fancy university for the name alone, parents should ask, *What education path will provide my kid with the chance to challenge themselves and grow as part of their education?*

There is no right way to parent or nurture. We want kids to be happy and secure, but above all we want them—at the appropriate time—to be fully engaged in reality. Life can be challenging. We cannot and should not be expected to be the best at everything we do. We have to be okay with failure. Kids need to develop resilience when faced with challenges and setbacks, and we should have conversations with them about dealing with failure.

By encouraging children to embrace obstacles, we can ensure that they become accountable for their actions. Accountability isn't just about outcomes. Whether we succeed or fail is often out of our control. But by orienting the conversation to what is under their control and whether they tried their best, we can equip a child with a mindset to best prepare them to achieve health, happiness, and financial independence. For parents, this is the greatest contribution they can make in raising resilient and capable children who can navigate a competitive and changing world.

Part 2
LEADERSHIP

IF YOUR ACTIONS INSPIRE OTHERS
TO DREAM MORE, LEARN MORE,
DO MORE, AND BECOME MORE,
YOU ARE A LEADER.

–JOHN QUINCY ADAMS

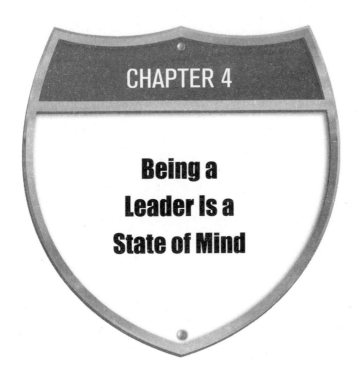

CHAPTER 4

Being a Leader Is a State of Mind

DEFINING TRAITS OF THE BUDDING LEADER: *The ability to influence and guide followers or members of an organization, society, or team to reach a common goal. Leaders are found and required in most aspects of society, including business, politics, religion, and social- and community-based organizations. Leaders are seen as people who make sound and sometimes difficult decisions. They articulate a clear vision, establish achievable goals, and provide followers with the knowledge and tools necessary to achieve those goals.*[13]

BEHAVIOR PATTERNS: *Leaders are confident, communicate effectively, manage themselves and others, and foster creative and innovative thinking. Leaders persevere in the face of challenges, are open to taking risks, and remain levelheaded. Leaders must be aware of themselves, their team, and the world around them, so that they can make informed decisions to ensure progress.*

LEADERSHIP IS A BROAD TERM because leaders are able to make an impact that extends beyond them to the groups and communities they serve. Leaders are often tested, which is why grit is so important. Leadership can require a person to believe in something bigger than themselves to be able to stay the course despite obstacles.

Leadership is critical for a young person to develop, but the ability to develop it has been challenged with the advent of social media and video games, which have made it easier for young people to prioritize themselves above the communities to which they belong. With social media, the instant gratification that comes from each response to a post encourages users to focus on themselves and how others perceive their actions. Users place themselves at the center of a universe that they create to elicit a response from others that drives feelings of self-worth. Perhaps it is no wonder that teens today report higher rates of loneliness relative to earlier generations. In fact, a study found that teenage loneliness worldwide had a 91 percent increase, from 16 percent to 31 percent from 2012 to 2018.[14]

With video games, young people receive a feedback loop that encourages them to retreat into an online world where the more they play, the further they progress. In either situation—social media or video games—teens are rewarded for focusing themselves on a pursuit that is tied neither to their communities nor their development as people.[15]

There's nothing wrong with enjoying solitary activities or focusing on ourselves. It is also important to recognize that, as individuals, we are all responsible for our commitments and we need to make sure that we handle them appropriately before even beginning to consider helping everyone else around us. And, yes, social media and video games can be fun. They are legitimate passions for influencers and gamers. But with that said, none of us lives on an island by ourselves. Our success and fulfillment as individuals are tied to the impact we make for others with respect to our education, careers, and personal lives.

To achieve success, young people need to understand that their ability to contribute to the world around them is what will define them. Mark Zuckerberg is not famous for starting a successful and valuable company. He is famous because he changed the way information is shared and how we communicate with one another through Facebook. Similarly, Jeff Bezos's reputation isn't built on being the wealthiest person on the planet but rather for transforming the way we shop through Amazon. For these entrepreneurs, their achievement and fame are not tied to their personal financial success but rather to how their actions positively impacted others. (Personal financial success is a nice bonus for creating something that betters people's lives.)

It is liberating to free ourselves from the idea that our success is stored simply within ourselves and not shared with others. Every young person who dreams of becoming successful by becoming an attorney, doctor, or coder could, if they wanted to, reframe their goals by saying, "I want to help others lead healthy lives," or "I want to be a legal advocate who helps people work through their problems," or "I want to build products that make difficult tasks easier."

By committing themselves to these types of goals, students can position themselves not just to be successful but to embrace a key trait that promotes success: becoming a *leader*.

Who Is a Leader?

When we think of leaders, U.S. presidents, CEOs, and professional sports coaches may come to mind. Within a typical school community, students may think of a class president, team captain, or club leader. Yes, all these people occupy leadership positions. But leadership is not solely confined to a title or role. It is a trait that defines people, their actions, and most importantly, their impact.

If we go back to the definition of leadership—"the ability to influence and guide followers or members of an organization, society, or team to reach a common goal"—nowhere does this description require a young person to run for student council or serve as a team captain. Leaders come in all shapes and sizes in their quest to help the organizations they belong to reach a common goal.

Young people today should embrace the fact that with the advent of technology, there is more room for them to be leaders in ways that are uniquely fitting for their individual strengths and personalities. Introverts may never need to face speaking to a packed auditorium to marshal their peers' talents together. They can make their pitch through e-mail or even, dare I say, social media. In the workplace, leaders can manage people in all corners of the globe due to instant communication platforms. They may never even need to be in the same room as their team. Whether at school or in the workplace, leaders need to develop a vision, a plan to execute it, and the ability to guide others toward that goal. This plan should reflect who they are and their leadership strengths.

Leadership isn't just for the outgoing or outspoken. Skilled at getting others engaged and believing in the cause? Great—you will probably succeed at being a visionary leader who occupies center stage. Excellent at making sure everything is completed? An effective leader can also work quietly in the background to ensure an organization executes its mission. There is space for every type of leader to contribute to an organization. A leader just needs to find their own way to do so. Along the way, if they can make the sum of the parts bigger than all the individuals, they will achieve success in their pursuits.

Leadership and College Admission

A college education is often considered the final step in a young person's development toward becoming an independent adult. It is the clear transition from a period when a minor is learning how to contribute to the period when they graduate and begin working or seeking more specialized higher education to continue on their path.

Colleges and the admissions officers they hire recognize that the students they admit and educate will one day graduate and become the brand ambassadors affiliated with their university. When stories of students starting tech platforms like Facebook or Microsoft in Harvard dorms emerge, Harvard's name attracts more young people and their parents, who hope that attending Harvard will allow them to emulate Zuckerberg's success (even if in some cases those students never actually graduate). Therefore, Harvard and other universities seek to admit applicants who demonstrate the potential to become leaders whose success stories will continue to draw students and strengthen the university's brand. This strategy of marketing is far more effective than any brochure.

Yale's website quotes its former president Kingman Brewster, who stated, "We have to make the hunchy judgment as to whether or not with Yale's help the candidate is likely to be a leader in whatever [they] end up doing." Brewster added, "We are looking for students we can help to become the leaders of their generation in whatever they wish to pursue."

In the much more immediate term, colleges also seek applicants with leadership capabilities because they view themselves as catalysts for their student populations, employees, and the communities that they serve. They seek to admit students who will propel their missions forward. This could include student leaders who are committed to helping vulnerable or marginalized populations surrounding the campus that can benefit from the transformative power of education. Others may inspire their classmates or fellow community members to work together for a cause that is greater than the institution itself. Whether it's voter registration drives or lobbying for policies that protect the community, admissions officers seek to admit students capable of making an impact while they attend their institutions. Admissions officers also want to enroll students who contribute to efforts like research or other forms of academic scholarship because universities position themselves as thought leaders. In addition, universities seek leaders who can support other members of their school communities in a time of need.

How do colleges evaluate leadership potential? They ask applicants to respond to questions along the lines of "What have you done to make your school or community a better place?" Aspiring applicants must recognize early on that this prompt will likely be the most frequently asked question in the college application process. To position themselves for success, not just in college admission but for their own personal development, students should take steps to develop leadership skills that reflect who they are.

The more an applicant is able to demonstrate the ability to make an impact as a leader, the stronger their odds of earning admission to colleges they seek to attend. It doesn't matter what type of leader the applicant develops into. From community organizer to CEO, universities want to build a class with a variety of interests and goals to extend that university's impact into vast segments of society. It doesn't matter where students' interests or skills as leaders lie; all that matters is that they make an impact.

A young person may think, *I have my whole life to develop into a leader. Why do I need to start in high school?* The answer is that you can never start too early. The greatest indicator of future potential is past performance. Anyone can say that they want to become a leader and have the *potential* to be an effective one. But talk is cheap in the college admissions process and most parts of life. Applicants who have already demonstrated their ability to make an impact provide more compelling evidence that they will do the same in college and beyond.

Leadership and Career Development

Young people have big dreams. No one's goal is to remain an entry-level employee for the rest of their life. Instead, they envision themselves as people who can make an impact, whether in a business-oriented career or a pursuit dedicated to helping people live healthier lives and contribute to medical advancements.

Regardless of the field, young people tend to romanticize their future careers and imagine themselves as changemakers in their organizations and communities. But a gap often exists between how they envision themselves and the work they actually contribute to an organization. It's easy to collect a paycheck by doing what is asked of you. But employees who show that they care and take steps to lead the company in a better direction are the ones who receive promotions.[16] Contributing to or fostering an organizational change leads to career advancement and accompanying pay raises.

Young people today need to possess the ability to assess, analyze, take action, and persuade a group to follow along if they hope to step into the leadership career roles they desire. Furthermore, the massive implications of artificial intelligence on the nature of work make it even more imperative that young people prove their worth by possessing a skill that machines don't: the ability to effectively manage people. Whoever can bring out the best in individuals and foster relationships that make an organization greater than the sum of its parts will have a lucrative job for life.

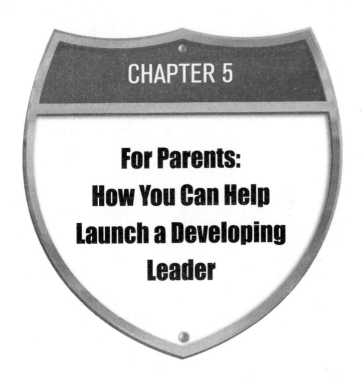

CHAPTER 5

For Parents: How You Can Help Launch a Developing Leader

THESE DAYS, EVERYONE IS BUSY—*especially* high school students. For those seeking to earn admission to selective colleges or prepare for life after they flee the nest, it is hard to find a student with time to spare as they juggle academics, sports, the arts, community service, clubs, and other extracurricular activities. Even as America grapples with a burnout culture, everyone is stacking their schedule with all the extracurriculars they can.

But this madness has a catch: Not everyone who is busy is investing their time in ways that are beneficial to them and achieving their long-term goals. Fortunately for college applicants, colleges are not just looking for students who are *busy*. Instead, colleges are seeking applicants who actually make a difference, instead of just showing up. The same is true of employers. For high school students with their eye on college, leadership translates into *making everything they do meaningful.*

In an era of 5 percent acceptance rates at sought-after public and private universities, résumé fillers do not differentiate an applicant from anyone else applying. Employers offering hard-to-land jobs are the same. Admissions officers and hiring managers alike are looking for applicants who have the potential to make an impact.

College applicants have mere sentences on their college applications to describe who they are and how they lead. Résumés and cover letters that follow for jobs after college are typically confined to one page each. As such, young people chasing their goals have very little space to prove that they are developing into effective leaders. With this in mind, they need to make sure that the experiences they participate in are not just busy work but actively contribute to their growth.

By intentionally focusing on cultivating leadership skills, we position ourselves to discover our strengths so that we can accomplish our goals. This approach also helps students avoid feeling overwhelmed or putting too much pressure on anything tied to college and career. The journey to college and career should be tied to the development of the whole person.

So, what does it mean to intentionally develop into leaders? The beauty of life is that each individual's journey to leadership is unique. For some who are born natural leaders, it is second nature to find opportunities to lead and harness each organization member's potential. But most young people could benefit from having a plan to develop into a leader, and that's where skillful parenting can help.

Let me be clear: I am not advising that you do things for your child so that they can achieve coveted positions as a club president or team captain. (In fact, I'll offer some very strong examples of why *not* to focus on titles.) But parents can and sometimes should step in to nudge their children in the right direction, to go from member to leader.

DO: Push your child to delve deeper and adopt a growth mindset.

I have met thousands of students who are bright, motivated, and promising young people. They dream of attending selective universities that they believe will help them achieve their goals. Many of them (and their parents) speak to me about their goals as if their ambitions alone equal qualifications.

With many students, I explain that the journey to a college and career rewards those promising young people who are capable of making an impact on an organization. How many students out there in the world have similar interests? The answer: Too many to count, and that is okay. Rather than worrying about a child's interests or who else shares them, parents can help their teens develop a growth mindset to pursue their interests and develop as leaders through them.

I met Luke as he entered his junior year of high school. Luke came to me with ambition. He had good grades, but that is where it ended. Luke told me he wanted to one day become an automotive engineer; he loved cars and followed Tesla news religiously. I explained to Luke that wanting to be the next Elon Musk would not be enough to make the case to admissions officers at UCLA, which was his dream school. After all, what car aficionado doesn't want to revolutionize the automobile industry? To really stand out, Luke would have to demonstrate his ability to grow by pursuing appropriate opportunities in a way that aligned with his interests.

Luke agreed to do so rather than look for shiny titles that sound exciting but don't translate to actionable potential and achievement. Instead of running for student government president, which sounds impressive but wasn't the right opportunity for him, Luke decided to get involved with his high school robotics team. Initially, he was just a member of the organization. But during his junior year, Luke learned how to wire an autonomous robot to power the drivetrain. Once he mastered the process, he began mentoring other members of the team and took on a de facto leadership role in assembling the robot's hardware. He didn't have a title, but he had the experience of teaching others and determining how to assign roles and responsibilities to achieve the team's goals. Because he had put in the work, he had many interesting experiences to write about in his college essays, and all of them demonstrated his ability to reflect thoughtfully on his own personal growth as a leader.

Best of all, Luke didn't just stop there. Eager to apply his love of cars with his newly licensed ability to drive, Luke decided to promote safe driving. Being on the introverted side, Luke preferred independent projects where he could work at his own pace and preferred style. Luke prioritized impact over club titles and began a social media campaign to emphasize the importance of not texting while driving. He asked the school to promote his content on their social media page and as a result generated thousands of impressions. He eventually decided to involve a few friends in the effort and invited car accident survivors to speak at lunchtime meetings.

Luke never intended to become a club president and didn't consider himself one. Robotics is offered at many high schools, and many sensible aspiring engineers start or join their high school robotics clubs. Luke's experiences were nothing out of the ordinary for many of today's high school students, but they were meaningful to him because they allowed him to grow through his interests. From a college admissions standpoint, they also spoke to a genuine interest in automotive technology and demonstrated his growth through his interest in the mechanical engineering programs that he applied to. While Luke was wait-listed at his top choice of UCLA, he was admitted to several strong programs. However, he declined his numerous acceptances and decided to study at the University of California, San Diego, because he wanted to live in a city that offered connections to automotive companies.

It should come as little surprise that as a college freshman, Luke began cold e-mailing several of the car design studios in San Diego near his campus and successfully secured an internship at one of the largest automotive companies in the world. In his e-mails and interviews, he referenced the joy he gained from building robots in high school and his belief that advancements in automotive technology could help keep people safe. This display of past accomplishments and promise to expand his skills and apply them to the industry made his internship inquiries successful.

Developing as a passionate leader was the catalyst Luke needed to pursue his dreams. It kept him honest about how he spent his time in high school and college. With infinite opportunities in life, he could hone in and focus on the ones that matter to him. Now, not everyone is as lucky as Luke was to know what interests them, especially at a young age. That is okay. Life is a constant process of trial and error. When one goal or interest doesn't come to fruition, we need to pivot and try something new. And this takes grit, which goes hand in hand with leadership skills.

A growth mindset allows students to focus on building their skills in ways that are relevant and meaningful to them and avoid viewing the college admissions process simply as a rat race. In the case of Luke, every activity he got involved with was a chance for him to explore, grow, and make a difference. He forged his own path as a result.

Students today need to try their best and put themselves out there to see what they enjoy and where they excel. Each failed attempt brings them closer to discovering what makes them tick. Even if they don't love every experience, learning how to inspire others and create change rewards them with critical life skills that admissions officers and hiring managers value.

Going back to Luke, his passion for cars is not what differentiated him from others when he was applying for internships. It was the fact that he was able to prove he was a leader in his community through his love of cars and demonstrate his potential to contribute to a car conglomerate. In his college applications, Luke wrote about his desire to promote safe driving as it is a serious problem for teens. But what helped Luke distinguish himself was that he was able to refer to an impact based on the impressions for his efforts promoting safe driving, the talks that he hosted, and the number of people he came in contact with through his endeavors. In short, Luke could prove his ability to affect others positively.

No matter our children's interests, we can help them find ways to make an impact. If they do not know what interests them, each growth experience allows them to discover what makes them tick, and how they can contribute to any organization that they are affiliated with or start.

Even if one's interests or goals change, the experiences gained from the desire to make an impact are transferable to other areas of life. Leaning into a genuine interest allows one's skill development to have meaning and relevance. In short, it makes work more fun and engaging for the person doing it.

This approach to growth is far superior to the mindset of checking boxes to build a résumé for an admissions officer or hiring manager. Such tasks will likely feel arbitrary and a chore to complete, and checking boxes will likely feel like arbitrary chores to complete, thereby hindering growth.

DON'T: Let your love for your child distort their reality.

Some parents allow their love for their children to cloud their objectivity when it comes to supporting them on the path to health, happiness, and financial independence. I lovingly refer to them as the *parents of special snowflakes*. To the parent of a special snowflake, whatever their child does makes them the greatest in the world. A special snowflake has no need for improvement because they are *so special* as is. But the fallacy of the special snowflake is that every snowflake is unique and therefore special.

Don't get me wrong, I love seeing parents' pride in their kids and their accomplishments. I also recognize that, to a parent, their child is the most special person in the world. Healthy parents, however, acknowledge that the world will likely not view their child in the same way—and for the child's sake, they try to push for meeting objective standards that measure the child's growth or impact.

A particularly intense parent of a special snowflake, Aileen, hired my team when her daughter, Kylie, was a high school freshman. In our first conversation, Aileen made it clear that she was looking for guidance for Kylie to earn admission to Yale or, if not Yale, then somewhere less selective like *[insert pause for dramatic effect here]* Columbia. Mind you, both schools accept around 1 to 2 percent of nonrecruited athletes or megalegacy students (i.e., the type of student whose parents donate enough money to have a building named for them).

As I do with every student who aspires to be admitted to Ivy or Ivy-equivalent schools, I made it clear as part of my consultation that admissions officers view research experience favorably because colleges are thought leaders that enhance our collective understanding of the world. The most selective schools in the country—like Yale— seek students who can contribute to the institution's thought leadership. Therefore, it would be in Kylie's best interest to identify and participate in research programs in which she could show her alignment with the school's goals.

So, when we began working with Kylie, we recommended a university-affiliated research program for high school students in which the snowflake student could explore her proclaimed interest in environmental justice and demonstrate an ability to contribute to academic research efforts. We thought this would be a great opportunity not only for Kylie's own personal development but also to help with her goals for college admission.

Instead of making a carefully considered decision to undertake or pass on applying for research opportunities, Aileen called to let me know that she would be hiring a different counselor for Kylie because our emphasis on the importance of research, which was outside of Kylie's interests, made it seem as though we did not value Kylie's accomplishments or see her strengths as an applicant. To hell with the fact that the schools Aileen dreamed of Kylie attending routinely reject 99 percent of applicants and that successful applicants need to develop the skills that college admissions officers are seeking.

With painstaking detail, Aileen began by reminding me that her child earned close to a perfect SAT test score. This is impressive, but as I had already told her, by no means is a top-shelf standardized test score a distinguishing factor when applying alongside the 95 percent of other applicants to Ivy League universities with equally perfect test scores.

Applicants need a competitive test score that meets the college's academic standards just to be *considered* for admission. Eager to defend Kylie as I pushed back on her insinuation that her SAT score would lead to admission, Aileen then rattled off *dozens* of different activities Kylie was involved with that spoke to her passion for climate change. I reminded Aileen that the college application only has room to list ten activities. Aileen then informed me that the mayor of their small city thanked Kylie for her efforts to promote recycling. While all this was great, the mayor's recognition would have zero impact with admissions officers. I asked Aileen how she thought her daughter should incorporate the thanks from the mayor, at which point she said, "Well, she can write about that in her essays."

My silence to that comment betrayed me: One instance of mayoral recognition would not translate into a deep and meaningful college essay. Aileen had arrived at the inner circle of college admissions hell: the reality that what one does may not make them special to others. Trapped, Aileen pivoted to what Kylie *wanted* rather than what she had *accomplished* by letting me know that Kylie is an environmentalist and feels strongly about decreasing the use of nonrenewable energy and single-use plastics.

Okay, but this process—and life, for that matter—doesn't revolve around what one's child thinks. Having beliefs and dreams is a start. Colleges, however, seek to admit applicants who put those beliefs and dreams into practice and make a difference. When it comes to applying to colleges, especially the Ivies, the admissions process rewards those who engage in experiences that demonstrate they are already developing the skills and perspective needed to add value to universities that have tens of thousands of applicants to pick from, all of whom are promising. As a private college counseling organization, we are here to provide honest feedback to help students make the case for admissions by giving the admissions officers *exactly* what they are looking for. Nothing more, and nothing less.

This is why I don't think being an environmentalist alone is what admissions officers prioritize. That many young people are concerned about climate change and environmental degradation is a safe assumption. At a personal level, I understand that many people do not believe in climate change, but again we want to emphasize an applicant's ability to add value to a college, which involves more than taking a stand on an important issue. That Kylie is an environmentalist is fantastic, but I am realistic enough to also recognize that considering one's child an environmentalist in and of itself is not sufficient for admission to an Ivy League university.

I am impressed with the passion that parents like Aileen convey for their children, but colleges need to find something compelling to offer a student admission, not just what Aileen finds compelling about her own daughter. But Aileen kept on by informing me that Kylie was at school every day until 9:30 PM. She didn't go to bed until 1:00 AM every day that week. She was confident she would have As in all her classes, with a GPA of 4.95 this semester—despite all the time she spent with dance and her volunteering.

Unfortunately, staying at school late doesn't qualify anyone automatically for anything. We don't *want* Kylie at school that late! What we actually want is for her to do what matters in this process and, from a personal standpoint, to get some sleep. It would also be nice if Aileen could recognize that 55 percent of college-bound high school students boast A grade point averages, so her GPA would not be a differentiating factor.

When it was time to face the elements, Kylie did not live up to familial expectations. Courtesy of the family that referred Aileen, we learned later that she was rejected by every one of the Ivy League universities she applied to. Adding more salt to the wound, she was also rejected from UCLA and UC Berkeley—her backup public universities, which have shockingly low acceptance rates as well.

Parents can avoid falling into the trap of placing their children on the pedestal of special snowflakes by encouraging them to develop objective frameworks to measure their impact. Rather than touting their interests, focus on measurable progress and distinctive accomplishments.

Parents should encourage their children to act upon their interests and assess their efforts based on the things they do that translate into easy-to-understand outputs. For example, a student interested in environmental conservation could organize efforts to place recycling bins in heavily trafficked areas of their school to avoid hundreds if not thousands of pounds of plastics from going to landfills. Then they could write about their efforts to protect the environment through that initiative when the time comes to apply to college. They can produce videos and post them on social media to urge their peers to skip the straw for their drinks and discuss the number of impressions they received from their campaigns. They can organize environmental cleanups for their school and write about how many peers joined the efforts.

While it is critical to nurture young people's goals and aspirations, parents should encourage their children to take concrete actions with measurable outcomes. While leading with their heart and goals, they should also take stock on a regular basis of what they are doing to live up to them. There are no right or wrong ways to make a difference. We just need to encourage future leaders to take the initiative now to step into what they hope to achieve. Each small action along the way eventually compounds into a journey that shows the ability to make an impact.

DO: Embrace your child for who they are, not what you want them to be.

Every parent has dreams for their child that run the gamut from becoming professionals like doctors or lawyers to achieving personal milestones like having families of their own someday. Along the way, parents can create their own narratives of what that should look like based on their perception of who they think their child should be rather than who they are.

Now this is not to say that a parent cannot or should not dream big for their child. A student who struggles with math or science in high school can still become a doctor or an engineer. Joe Biden's childhood stutter probably got in the way of his becoming student council president, but it didn't stop him from becoming president of the United States.

Parents need to balance their hopes and dreams for their children with the child's strengths and interests. Encouraging them to explore different areas and guiding them to develop skills or perspectives that a parent thinks are crucial to their development is healthy and normal. But when a parent's hopes or dreams replace the child's, a problem arises.

The child's life is not for the parent to live. The parent's role is to help the child grow and develop so that they have the foundation to achieve their goals. False starts, stumbles, and roadblocks along the way are okay. The life experience they gain from those trying circumstances empower them to succeed on their terms when the time is right.

Each child should be encouraged to develop skills and perspectives that are meaningful to their interests. Forcing a child who has no interest in the healthcare field to volunteer at a hospital will not magically make them interested in becoming a healthcare provider. A parent who has visions for their child to demonstrate athletic prowess and leadership on the soccer field when the child dislikes soccer will not see that child rise to the challenge to become team captain.

Rather than forcing children to participate in activities that do not align with their interests, parents can help their children discover what makes them tick by requiring them to engage in activities that help them become leaders in areas that interest them. This does not mean a child who is interested in nothing beyond watching YouTube videos and TikTok reels should be allowed to scroll incessantly on their phones. This simply means giving the child a choice of how they spend their time in a productive way. This will empower them to dedicate themselves to causes and activities that are meaningful to them and inspire them to make an impact when they feel they have the agency to apply themselves and live up to their full potential.

A student I once worked with embodies this lesson fully. Trevor began with me the summer before ninth grade. He was on the smaller side and soft-spoken. His parents initially thought that he had to play a sport in high school to be admitted to college (more of why this is not true to come in Part 3). Trevor hated tennis. He admitted he wasn't very good at it, and it affected his confidence and self-worth playing with kids who were much better than him.

Instead of enhancing his high school career, forcing tennis on Trevor actually worked to his detriment. His entire freshman year was consumed with arguments between Trevor and his parents, and their argument often relied on college admission. Trevor did make the freshman-level team but did not play much and struggled during tennis season to complete all his homework and study sufficiently for tests. He procrastinated, and his grades suffered.

Trevor mustered up the courage the summer after his freshman year to ask his parents to quit tennis. They asked him what he wanted to do with his time instead, and his answer shocked them to the point where they insisted on an emergency counseling session with me: He wanted to play video games.

Every parent of a teenager obsessed with video games reading this is probably rolling their eyes and acknowledging their own struggles with getting their gamer off the screen and back into the real world.

In the counseling session, they asked Trevor how colleges would look at his decision to quit tennis. They followed up with a question about what he would write about for his college essays. "Playing video games?", they wondered aloud and waited for Trevor to respond.

I encouraged Trevor to come up with an answer to his parents' question and find a way to show his growth through video games if that is what he wanted to do. He asked his parents for time to come up with a plan. If he could find a way to make video games work for him, they would allow him to quit tennis.

Normally, getting Trevor to do anything in life was a bit of a struggle, so I was surprised that within a few short weeks, I received an e-mail from him requesting to meet. Attached to his e-mail was a PowerPoint presentation. He had formed a plan.

Through online research, Trevor discovered the nascent but fast-growing arena of esports. Trevor wanted to form an esports team at his high school. He would recruit other gamers, seek sponsorships to enter into tournaments, and teach his teammates game strategy so that they could improve their performance. While I admit I am personally not a fan of video games, I saw a spark in Trevor's eyes that I had never seen. He seemed genuinely excited about the idea, and his plan did feature the underpinnings of leadership.

I asked Trevor to include a community service component to his team to show that he is capable of making an impact on his community through his love of gaming. He agreed to plan esports tournaments in which the entry fees would serve as fundraisers to purchase toys for local children's hospitals. He even pitched a local gaming company their idea, and they agreed to purchase additional toys to give to the hospital.

Trevor's esports team grew to be one of the largest outside-of-school activities at his high school. They did well in tournaments and raised over $1,000 for the local children's hospital. He became more efficient with his studying and homework because he knew that he had to do well in school to keep gaming and working with his team. His grades improved as a result.

When the time came to apply to college, Trevor wrote about having to convince his parents, his school, and his community about his idea. He wrote about being true to himself and the skills he developed along the way doing something that most people view "as a waste of time." He wrote about how it made him appreciate the underdog in any situation and the need to advocate for them.

In his first year of undergrad, Trevor e-mailed me to tell me that he wanted to go to law school and be an advocate for others. I was ecstatic. All because he had to fight to do what he loved: playing video games. He is now studying environmental science and hopes one day to ensure that more is done to protect the environment. He still games for fun but recognizes that he needs to keep his grades up in college so that he can get into law school. Trevor may be the ultimate success story when it comes to gaming. It gave him perspective, the chance to develop his advocacy and leadership skills, and the opportunity to apply his leadership journey in a way that was appropriate and made an impact in a way that was meaningful to him. His parents, while understandably skeptical about gaming as a career prospect at first, appreciated that gaming allowed Trevor to develop the skills he needed to reach his potential while also pursuing his hobbies and passions.

While not every gamer will have this same journey, it is important to recognize that every child can find ways to make an impact and grow through their interests. By allowing children to find the way to apply themselves in what feels right or natural to them, they can achieve key developmental milestones that prepare them for what comes next in their lives.

Parents can and should give their children the option to choose activities or causes that are meaningful to them. Rather than focus on the activity, hold them accountable for finding ways to grow in their pursuits. The growth, regardless of the field, is what will empower them to succeed in the future.

As Trevor's story demonstrates, parents can insist that their kids tie activities they engage with to service, like tournaments to raise money for charity. Any activity that involves other people, whether in person or online, presents a young person with the chance to find ways to bring out the best in an organization. Insist that the child optimize what they are affiliated with because that experience is what helps them grow—and that growth is what will transfer to other areas of their life.

DON'T: Force it.

Everyone develops as a leader at a different pace and in different ways. Life rewards those capable of staying true to themselves and their unique interests. The world is more competitive than ever, and it seems like fewer opportunities are available for young people relative to earlier generations. No matter the state of the world, those who can find their own niche that caters to their strengths and interests will be rewarded.

Children today feel less stress and more inspiration if they find their own unique paths. They need not feel like they are competing with the entire world if they are simply competing to be the best version of themselves and doing the best they can to achieve their goals.

With that said, no young person or their parents ever needs to compare their achievements or path to others' unique paths. Just because Timmy down the street is involved with the Science Olympiad or Susy who lives in the next town over started a club doesn't mean that one's own child should be pursuing the same activity. If it is not relevant to their journey, it won't benefit them.

Early one morning, I received a frantic text message from a parent named Nancy asking me to call her as soon as possible. It was barely 7:00 AM, and the timing made me worry that something was wrong. I called her, and at what sounded like the point of tears, Nancy exclaimed that several of her son Ian's friends had applied to a coding internship at a nearby university, and she was furious that her son had not applied to the same program. *How dare I not inform them of this opportunity!*

I was dumbfounded. I am all for young people exploring their passions and believe that coding skills are useful for all young people today, given the role technology will continue to play in all aspects of our lives. However, Nancy's son took computer science at school and disliked the class immensely. He had no plans to study computer science in college or pursue a career in the field.

"Nancy, how is a coding internship supposed to help your son?" I asked.

"Well, he needs internships to be admitted to a selective college to show he is learning, growing, and contributing," she responded.

It is great that Nancy recognized the importance of internships as a way to show an applicant's ability to contribute to an organization bigger than themself, but this particular program had no relevance for Ian. For Ian to make the case for admission and later for a job, he would have to show that he was growing in ways relevant to his journey and goals.

Even with my explanation, Nancy wasn't buying it. "Well, surely this opportunity would have looked good to the schools on his list!"

I reminded Nancy that college applications would ask Ian how he explored *his* academic interests outside the classroom and what and why he wanted to study at specific universities. It would be hard to make the case for his interest in biology by writing about learning how to debug software with aspiring coders.

Nancy was still incensed that her son hadn't applied to the program, and her bitterness that he had not applied to the program underscored what felt like her true issue with the situation: Other kids her son's age whom she viewed as her son's competition were applying for opportunities that Ian wasn't. Even if the growth opportunity wasn't relevant for her son, if others were pursuing it, she thought, so should Ian.

However, pursuing an internship in a field that Ian wasn't interested in would deprive him of the chance to find other ways to contribute to an organization or cause that was meaningful and relevant to him. Time is our most precious resource at any stage of our lives, and I wanted Ian to use his time wisely to help him grow.

Parents should help their kids prioritize their ability to make an impact and acquire skills that they, and they alone, will need in the future. Doing so takes the stress off the child to spread themselves thin and reorient their mindset to grow in their own unique way.

We can encourage kids to find a cause that they find worthy of their time rather than as a passion or a career path. By framing it as "Do you want to spend your time doing this?," students can approach any growth opportunity as a chance to develop passion and skills they will rely on later. For students anxious about committing themselves to something they are unsure about, encourage them to "get involved" rather than "find a way to be a leader." If the fit is there and they enjoy the activity, they will find a way to grow into a leader for that activity. For parents worried about whether their child is doing "enough" for college applications, reorient the conversation to doing something to help someone else in need. The applicant's ability to make an impact is what will demonstrate their perspective and leadership potential. Along the way, framing every opportunity as a chance to build skills and make a difference can help young people develop the initiative and drive to emerge into the types of civically minded leaders whom admissions officers and employers covet for their organizations.

Dedicating ourselves to causes we believe in and using that as an objective framework to avoid unnecessary activities that add to our stress can help students avoid widespread problems with burnout. Fifty-one percent of teens say that, at least once a month, someone has told them that they seem stressed or burnt out. Many report that during the school year they have an average stress level of 5.8 on a 10-point scale, compared with a level of 4.6 during the summer.[17] Sticking with causes they believe in teaches students how to prioritize their time as adults when they will also be tasked with juggling personal and professional commitments that can be even more demanding.

Avoiding burnout and developing leadership skills are critical not just for the journey to college but for careers too. Today, three in four employers say they have a hard time finding graduates with the soft skills (e.g., critical thinking, problem-solving, and interpersonal and communication skills) that their companies need.[18] Prioritizing skill acquisition as a leader allows young people to develop these critical skills that they will rely on for the rest of their lives.

In a labor market increasingly defined and potentially limited by automation and artificial intelligence, leadership skills will become increasingly important for young people seeking to advance in their careers. Seventy-three percent of hiring managers reported that communication skills are important to gaining leadership positions at their organization, while 75 percent reported listening as crucial. A further 74 percent reported critical thinking skills as important, and to round out the top four, 73 percent listed interpersonal skills.[19] Easily automated skills, such as quantitative reasoning and computer skills, are less in demand. While important, these skills alone don't necessarily translate into leadership capabilities. This is precisely why high school students today cannot expect to grow simply by being a club or organization member where they carry out tasks that others assign. While not everyone can be a leader in all their activities, young people need to identify and prioritize opportunities in which they can lead so that they can develop the skills they will require throughout their lives.

While we never should force leadership or growth opportunities when they are not a fit, we must be committed to finding ways to make an impact. Prioritizing what is meaningful to a person allows them to have the time and energy to pursue opportunities when they arise.

Learning how to advocate for what one believes in to start a club or convince others of the importance of paying attention while driving are two of the first steps students featured in this section accomplished to gain critical communication and interpersonal skills. Rather than obsessing over impressing college admissions officers, these students were rewarded with desired outcomes because they developed skills they can apply later in their lives. Admissions officers recognized this in these students. But far more important than college admission, these students and other equally committed peers are developing the skills and perspective they need to advance as leaders in whatever they do.

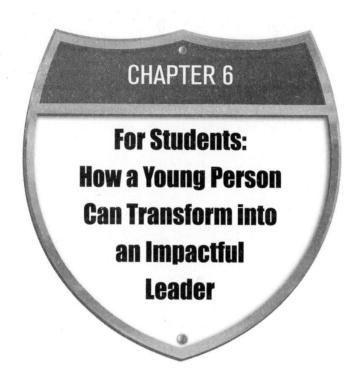

CHAPTER 6

For Students: How a Young Person Can Transform into an Impactful Leader

THE JOURNEY TOWARD COLLEGE AND A CAREER measures your growth and potential to contribute to an organization. It's not about what an applicant has done, but what they have learned and how they can apply that to what comes next in their life.

Said differently, for the foreseeable future, the journey is more important than the destination. Discovering what you love to do and how to do it will propel you to achieve your hopes and dreams.

Our interests may and should change over time. The careers of tomorrow may not exist today, and the most sought-after industries or positions right now may become irrelevant in the future. Young people need to be flexible and adapt to changes. Focusing exclusively on a specific path in life can inhibit them from developing into someone who can seize the right opportunity when the time arises.

By focusing on developing as a leader, you can position yourself to try new things, see what feels good, and explore based on this experience. If you are enjoying a certain activity or experience, build upon that. Interested in engineering? Join the robotics club. Are you told that you would make a great lawyer because you argue rather well with Mom and Dad? Try mock trial. Don't be afraid to get your hands dirty. Only by exploring new things and having new experiences are you able to truly tell where your skills lie and how to apply your interests in a way that resonates with you. Being an ER doctor might look great on paper and TV, but until you've volunteered at a hospital and seen if you enjoy the high-pressure environment of emergency care and can physically and emotionally tolerate blood and pain, you won't know if it is truly your calling. If you find that it's not, keep pivoting until you find a better fit.

Admissions officers seek applicants who show an ability to make a positive impact in their communities. They are not tied to a specific type of activity or cause; all they want to see is a person who is applying themselves to make a difference. There are no right or wrong ways to do this. Admissions officers measure the perspective an applicant has gained from an experience through their application essay. This means that *how* an applicant chooses to make an impact is secondary to the importance of (a) *making* an impact and (b) *growing* through that impact.

When it comes to advancing in a career, every person as part of their job is required to carry out certain responsibilities or tasks.

Many of them can be learned on the job or through training. But advancing in an organization requires us to be leaders who can further the organization's mission. Yong people today should develop a growth mindset and commit themselves to becoming leaders.

Your development is what will empower you to succeed despite working on other people's terms. Any chance to learn, grow, and try new things helps you develop the skills and perspective that you need to grow into who you want to become. Whether you are in high school, college, or just starting your career, commit to becoming a leader in a way that is appropriate to who you are and who you want to be.

DO: Take a chance on yourself.

It is always a bit nerve-racking to put ourselves out there. Anything we do comes with the risk that it might not work out the way we hope. Anxiety about outcomes and concern about whether we will succeed is universal. An estimated 35 percent of young people feel anxious about the future.[20] Even the most successful people worry about what's down the road, but what separates them from those who do not achieve their goals is a willingness to try to see what happens.

Before letting self-doubt consume us, we should ask ourselves, *What is the worst that could happen?* Think about this for a minute. The answer should be nothing. What is the worst that can happen if we run for student council and do not win? Or try to become a team captain but come up short? Absolutely nothing. You may feel you've wasted your time, but at least you know for sure what you can improve on, or maybe you find out what you don't want to pursue, and you can put your time into other activities with more potential. Learning how to promote oneself through a sports campaign or figuring out a way to demonstrate an ability to lead a team are both valuable lessons that prepare any person for new opportunities in the future. But we also have to be prepared to fail, fail, and fail some more. With self-reflection and a growth mindset, we can transform every failure into a chance to fail forward.

Some of the greatest leaders in a variety of fields failed on their paths. Abraham Lincoln famously lost multiple congressional elections before being elected president of the United States. Every hard-fought campaign in Illinois that did not send him to Washington prepared him for the grueling national campaign to become president. Even Bill Gates started and failed with Traf-O-Data before successfully launching Microsoft. Had Lincoln and Gates not tried their hands with politics or software development, respectively, they likely would not have developed the skills and perspective needed to preserve the Union in the Civil War or transform the world during the information age.

At a bare minimum, we must be open to trying new things. Even if we don't succeed or even enjoy the experience, we can learn incredible things about ourselves and the world. We can discern whether we like managing people, what our management styles are, and how we feel best suited to make a difference. Embrace the unknown and where it may lead. By keeping an open mind, we learn and prepare ourselves for whatever comes next.

Skills are forged through our experiences. We have to give ourselves the chance to develop them. Just as importantly, it's hard to truly know what we enjoy or are good at unless we put ourselves out there. Many impactful leaders' full potential was not known until they were in a position where they were called upon to act and lead.

President Lyndon Johnson, prior to being elected vice president, served as a U.S. senator from Texas. Johnson was able to break the filibuster by his fellow southern Democrats of the Civil Rights Act of 1964 by working with northern Democrats and liberal Republicans to pass the monumental legislation. Few at the time expected this incredible leadership to emerge from an unlikely source, given LBJ's Southern roots. Even in more modern times and outside the realm of politics, some of the most influential companies were started not with the intention to disrupt industries but just to make ends meet.

Airbnb founder Brian Chesky did not imagine his idea to host travelers in his apartment in graduate school would evolve into a multibillion-dollar behemoth that has changed the way we travel. His leadership emerged not with the idea he had, but his ability to make a couch for rent and a Pop Tart breakfast into a company that influenced our culture. Until any of us are called to make an impact, we do not know what we are capable of doing as a leader.

I once worked with a student, Tyler, whose family moved right before the start of high school. He knew no one in the new city where he lived or the school he would attend and was worried that he would struggle to make friends and get involved. The first several months of high school were rough, and he felt left out. Truth be told, he was left out. Cliques had formed in middle schools long before the first day of class, and he didn't know what clubs to join or activities to get involved with as nothing seemed that interesting to him. He ended up watching a lot of movies with his family at home on the weekends.

I encouraged Tyler to volunteer on his own by himself at a few places near where he lived to understand the unmet needs in his community. But Tyler didn't want to volunteer alone, and I understood that as well. I encouraged Tyler to view volunteering as a chance to discover his interests. A local health clinic could expose him to the world of medicine, while a food bank would teach about economic inequality. While acknowledging that both of these offered vital services to those in need, argument after argument erupted between Tyler and his mom because, ultimately he didn't want to wake up early on Saturday to go to either of them and assist, even if it would also help him with college admission. He is not the only teenager who would rather sleep in.

While Tyler and his mom were fighting like cats and dogs over his lack of involvement in school and the community, he was fulfilling his high school art requirement through his video film class. He enjoyed the class immensely. It allowed him to create his own stories. Just as important for his happiness, it was collaborative, and he was getting to meet new people and work with them. He started making friends in class.

Hearing the way Tyler talked about his film class was great. I enjoyed listening to his descriptions of the film editing process, and he didn't mind poring over the film content and making sure it was perfect. He sounded completely different talking about film rather than serving food at the soup kitchen.

Tyler's mom asked how he could translate his budding passion for film into developing and demonstrating leadership. Expecting me to back her up and tell her and Tyler there was no way, I told Tyler it would be up to him to find a way to be a leader through his film. I suggested to Tyler that he volunteer at the local soup kitchen to see the work they do and support them. Perhaps while volunteering he could offer to make videos to highlight hunger in the community to raise awareness and encourage people to donate food and funds to further their cause. Tyler asked, "What if they say no to my offer to make videos for them?" My answer for him was "So what? You can volunteer at other nonprofits until you find one that is interested in collaborating with you." With that mindset, Tyler actually wanted to wake up early and give it a shot.

The first time he volunteered at the soup kitchen, he approached the director and pitched her his free services. Desperate for additional funds, she wholeheartedly agreed to post the videos he would produce on their Facebook page. Tyler saw the importance of volunteering there regularly so that he could capture the stories of the patrons. He wanted to understand their needs and develop a story that would hopefully inspire others to give. Tyler produced a series of videos for the soup kitchen over the course of several years. He also volunteered regularly to help out with meal prep, serving, and cleaning. Tyler may not have realized this at the time, but he was becoming a leader in his community.

Tyler felt empowered to offer his filming services to other nonprofits in his community and over time built a brand around his ability to make a difference through his art. With confidence, Tyler began writing more scripts, entering film contests, and helping out with his school's student government to promote their upcoming events. Tyler found his groove and he flourished.

Tyler became a leader because he was willing to try something new and focused more on developing his skills rather than focusing on finding a way to make an impact. By tying the two together, he found a path that was enjoyable to him and enabled him to help others at the same time.

Putting himself out there and trying to tie his interest in film to serving his community also allowed Tyler to discover his true passion for filmmaking. Tyler developed an impressive résumé with which he could show project management skills, a gift for story-telling, and an ability to contribute to his community.

He was admitted to one of the top film programs in the United States at the University of Southern California, which is just a stone's throw away from Hollywood. The film program is known for molding the creators of famous TV shows and movies. Now a college student, Tyler wants to become a film producer, which is essentially the person who manages all aspects of film production. He hopes to be finding locations, securing actors, supporting directors, and raising funds to make films. He wants to have the ultimate leadership position within the film industry because he enjoys being a leader in an industry that is right for him. His mom is thrilled knowing that he is leading through his passion for film and has a plan for his future as a result.

To discover our paths and build the skills we need to navigate them, we all have to take a chance and see what feels right. Even if we stumble along the way, we learn how to make an impact. There is nothing wrong with stopping something that doesn't feel good, but we always have to keep trying to find the right fit. When we do find that match, the skills we gain will allow us to make an impact and grow as people and leaders.

Each young person should embrace being relentless when it comes to their own life—seeking out ways to grow, improve, or find a niche. Never settle for "No," "I don't know," or "We'll see." Refuse to settle when it comes to your life, and embrace that the journey will be the means to discover what you excel at and what you enjoy doing. When you find your path, it will feel natural and you will be able to apply what you have learned to make a far bigger impact, which will be what propels you to success.

DON'T: Overextend yourself.

Our most precious resource in life at any age is not money. It's time. Whether we are in high school and struggling to find the time to study, hang out with friends, and be involved, or as adults when we are balancing careers with our personal lives, we all simply run out of enough time to do the things we need to do, should be doing, and would like to be doing.

Recognizing that time is our most precious resource encourages us to make the most of it. Young people are more than accustomed to hearing a parent tell them to "stop wasting time," especially when it comes to doing homework and getting off social media. I would like to reframe it around a different approach. Every person—young, old, or somewhere in between—should spend their time wisely. Adopt a growth mindset with how you use your time. Use it well, use it for good, and use it on yourself.

As mentioned before, life rewards those who are able to make a meaningful difference for the causes or activities that matter the most to them. No one is able to do that if they don't give themselves the time to do so. When it comes to college, most applications only allow students to list up to ten activities in which they are involved. Colleges thus put a premium on the quality of the experiences rather than their quantity. The same is true with a résumé used for applying to jobs. Most hiring managers prefer to see a one-page résumé for an applicant's *entire* career. They want to see skills and experiences relevant to the roles for which they are recruiting. Again, when it comes to a résumé or job application, what matters the most is the quality and the development of skills and perspectives that are relevant and in demand for the person evaluating the application.

As a result, we need to give ourselves the time to grow through the experiences to which we commit. We may be tempted to sign up for as many activities as we can, thinking it will stack our résumés and make us seem more accomplished—but remember, what we do with each experience is what actually matters. In an era when most high school students report feeling burned out on a monthly basis, overcommitting to too many activities or responsibilities deprives a person of the chance to make a meaningful contribution to the ones that matter the most. Said differently, stretching ourselves thin can prevent us from developing as impactful leaders.

I started working with a student named Maggie prior to the start of her senior year of high school. Maggie's mom told me that she had "a perfect résumé." I wasn't sure what that meant but was surprised to see that it was three pages long. Maggie had started four clubs and was involved in numerous other activities including student council, field hockey, and her church. Somewhere between all these activities she also found time to play the piano. Way to go, Maggie!

Maggie looked like a leader on paper, but something wasn't adding up. I asked how long she was spending on each of the activities listed on her résumé while still managing to study for school and presumably sleep just a bit every night. She confided in me that when it came to many of the activities on her résumé, she wasn't doing anything at all. "I want colleges to see that I am a leader by being so involved," she exclaimed when reviewing her engagements.

So I followed up with a simple question about how she could demonstrate she was being a leader through her various clubs and other activities. She kept returning to the fact that she had started four clubs. I kept trying to drill down by asking what she was doing in each club beyond registering it with her school. She admitted that with everything she had going on, she only had time to have one monthly lunch meeting for each of the four clubs.

Since Maggie was focused on earning admission to highly selective colleges, I framed the problem in a way that I hoped she would understand. I explained to her that the college applications ask students to reflect upon how they made a difference in their community, not what their roles were. She could write that she started a club, but what would truly set her apart would be showing that the club(s) she started made a difference and what she learned by making that difference.

Maggie looked at me dumbfounded when I asked her to discuss the impact of the lunch meetings she was hosting. Her mom followed up with an e-mail accusing me of making her daughter feel unaccomplished in high school. To be clear, the conversation is not about accomplishments but rather impact. I wanted Maggie to learn how to prioritize impact over titles, as this would empower her to succeed in the college application process and beyond. Maggie ended up submitting college essays that discussed how she started multiple clubs. She did not write much about the impact these clubs made because there wasn't much to say.

Maggie had incredible grades and test scores to accompany her three-page résumé. Many would assume that she would earn admission wherever she applied. However, she was rejected by all her colleges except for the two safety schools that she applied to whose academic standards were significantly lower than her GPA and ACT score. She underperformed with her applications. Fortunately, Maggie's backups are amazing schools with incredible opportunities for young people to develop the skills and perspective they need for their futures.

I share Maggie's college admissions results not just to frame it within the college admissions process but to show how being over-involved doesn't necessarily lead to the outcomes we hope for in any capacity in our lives. Perhaps if Maggie had stuck to starting just one club and spent the time she used on the other three clubs to volunteer and harness her classmates' potential, she would have been able to point to a meaningful impact in her community. The growth from making an impact through the sole club may have provided her with more to reflect upon in her college application essays and resulted in more favorable outcomes.

Whether this is applied to education, our careers, or our personal lives, if we have too much on our plates, we won't be able to do what we need to do well enough to make a meaningful impact that will define who we are or speak to our potential. Rather than building a list of activities whose titles are meant to impress others, we should prioritize developing skills and perspectives that can demonstrate our ability to make an impact.

To do this, we need to give ourselves the time necessary to learn and grow through each experience we've committed to. If this requires us to pare down our commitments, that is a good thing! It will result in less stress and more chances to grow.

Make a plan for each week with how you want to spend your time. Time is precious, so you want to make the most of it. If the goal is to tackle hunger in your community, ask what that looks like. Volunteering at a food bank once or twice a month? There isn't a right answer; it just needs to be more significant than a monthly meeting at school where people talk about the issue for a few minutes before scrolling through social media. By setting a goal and the time it takes to achieve it, you create a path to make an impact. The person spending the time making a difference will be rewarded through their personal growth and for the impact they make that affects the lives of others.

Part of spending time wisely is knowing when to say no or to quit when something has run its course or no longer is meaningful. Quitting something or prioritizing another activity or experience can free up time that can be harnessed more effectively. Be prepared to reflect on your progress and satisfaction from any activity. While every activity will not always feel good all the time, if it isn't bringing you closer to your goals, or you feel stretched too thin, reflecting will allow you to reorient yourself to what matters the most at that moment.

Prioritize what is the most important. Put on the back burner the commitments that are inhibiting you from enjoying life. Focus on what you would like to do based on your interests, or what you need to do to grow to achieve your next slate of goals.

The hardest part of becoming an adult is learning how to balance all that competes for our time. You will only get busier. Being busy is only worth it if you put your time and energy into meaningful activities with the potential to help you reach your goals. Only then will you feel that you are working toward a destiny that's bigger than high school and college.

DO: Build upon achievable milestones.

Many of our ultimate goals are the result of years of hard work and dedication, with many steps along the way. Graduating from college also requires graduating from high school and middle and elementary school. People who dream of starting a business may need to set goals like learning how businesses operate before they embark on that path as well.

Whatever the goal, many steps are necessary to get there. Our success is defined by our ability to reach and realize our goals. This process requires tenacity and commitment. Completing the small steps along the way empowers a person with a sense of accomplishment and prevents them from feeling overwhelmed by the challenges and duration the ultimate goal demands.

As an example, what if I asked a student to run a marathon? Dropping the student off at the starting point and saying, "Good luck," would feel incredibly daunting for the student. Where does one begin? All the student would be able to think is, *Do I really need to run the entire thing?* But if I were to start the student by running one lap around the track, and then two the next day, and they gradually trained to run a marathon over the course of a few months, the marathon, while still a challenge, would feel much more manageable.

Our lives are marathons. We are in it for the long haul. Everything we want to accomplish will take time. It will take even more effort along the way. We do not need to stress about the final outcomes but should challenge ourselves to make progress every step of the way to reach the milestones we need to hit to eventually get there. There may be stumbles along the way, but if we trip at mile 2, does it matter if our goal is to run the entire 26.2 miles? As long as we can pick ourselves up and keep going, the answer is a resounding no.

The same is true with the journey to developing as a leader. An aspiring tech entrepreneur may dream of building the next Meta or Amazon and see themselves on the same magazine covers as Mark Zuckerberg or Jeff Bezos. But before they get there, they need to learn technical skills, develop an understanding of how technology can transform our lives, identify an opportunity, execute, and finally, scale their product so that it becomes a common and integral part of our lives. Easier said than done, and there are countless steps along the way to get there.

Young leaders with the potential to make an impact need to find causes they believe in. They need to figure out a way to get involved, and when they do, they must learn how to get others involved to enhance their impact and make a bigger difference. This could mean starting a club, or joining an existing organization and spearheading an effort to expand it, or it may look completely different from either of those options. The actual steps matter far less than the fact a person is taking them.

Taking small, actionable steps allows us to hold ourselves accountable for reaching the milestones. We can set concrete timelines to achieve them. If we were to give ourselves six months to get an organization off the ground and make a difference, at what point in those six months would we say we are behind or not meeting our expectations? It is hard to say.

However, if the same aspiring leader were to give herself two weeks to find a nonprofit organization to partner with, another two weeks to recruit other board officers, two weeks to make a website, and two weeks to secure a venue, would it not be much easier to keep track of those steps? Each bit of progress would provide an additional sense of accomplishment that would further propel the leader to keep going to reach the ultimate goal. If the leader would need to change course along the way, the differentiable steps would allow her to isolate the challenge and correct that specific part without altering the overall plan too.

A student leader I know who exemplified the importance of completing small, actionable steps to develop into an impactful leader is Matteo. Matteo enjoyed math and physics when he was in high school and expressed an interest in eventually becoming a mechanical engineer when he first met with me.

Matteo knew that he enjoyed working with and helping younger kids from his years of babysitting for families in his neighborhood. I encouraged him to start tutoring kids at a school in an underserved part of his community where most of the parents did not have high school degrees or speak enough English to help their kids with their education.

As he began tutoring elementary school students in math, he saw a huge need for academic support. He also realized it extended far beyond his local community. When the COVID-19 pandemic hit, Matteo couldn't tutor in person anymore. He offered remote lessons via Zoom but was inundated with so many requests that he couldn't keep up.

So Matteo decided to create a YouTube channel to teach elementary and middle school math and science. But a lot of math and science concepts are covered over years of school, and if Matteo were to say, "I am going to create a channel that helps kids," the goal would have been too vague and too big for him to feel capable of tackling.

Instead, Matteo committed himself to recording one math and one science lesson per week. To make it more specific and impactful, I encouraged him to find a way to make it relatable and enjoyable to kids. We developed a plan to apply his passion for soccer. He used ball flight to explain angles in geometry and his soccer cleats to illustrate the concept of friction.

But Matteo's work was just beginning to make his YouTube channel impactful. The next step was developing a plan to get the word out there. Matteo decided to spend two weeks researching elementary and middle schools online where students could benefit from the content he was creating. Once he compiled the list, he decided to send a few e-mails each week introducing himself to principals, assistant principals, and math and science teachers letting them know about his videos. He made it easy on himself to actually reach the weekly goals so that he could stay motivated every step of the way. Rather than sending hundreds of e-mails, Matteo studied which e-mails got the best responses from schools and modified his approach to make it more effective.

When the time came to apply to college, Matteo wrote about using the scientific method to test out his method of communication when it came to sending e-mails and how he believed thinking like an engineer made him a more effective leader who was capable of expanding the reach of his program. He was admitted to his top-choice college: Carnegie Mellon University, which has one of the most respected and sought-after engineering programs in the United States.

Regardless of their goals, individuals can create their own paths to make an impact by laying out a series of small and short-term wins to power them along. Whether it's doing an hour's worth of research for potential organizations, sending e-mails, or creating a plan with key steps to make an impact, the idea is to avoid doing something that seems abstract or too much to tackle. With each completed task, a developing leader can create a positive feedback loop to stay inspired and committed to the end goal. The impact will follow with the progress made.

DON'T: Rely on puffery.

How fancy something sounds on paper matters far less for our lives in the real world if whatever it means or does is inconsequential. Empty titles are often referred to as *puffery*. They puff someone or something up on paper, but when one peels back the outer layers of it, it becomes apparent that the puffery has little or no substance.

Think of someone who calls themself a company CEO when they are the sole employee. Yes, they are the chief executive officer, but the title means little when there isn't an organization to manage. Starting a club in high school that actually does little could also be considered puffery.

When the time comes to apply to college or a job, or to pitch investors to start a business or a foundation for a research grant, people are evaluated based on their skills and experiences, not their titles. Yes, titles are often associated with experience and skills. A director of an organization typically has experience managing people. A director with experience managing people can talk specifically about that background in an interview or list key responsibilities on their résumé that will help someone else evaluate their capabilities. Puffery becomes a problem when someone calls themself a director but has no direct reports. In that case, the title means nothing, yet the so-called director still seeks positions or opportunities suited to people who have the experience and skills, not just the titles.

While students still have a ways to go before committing puffery in the workplace, it may start during their education and college applications when it comes to extracurricular activities. Being involved in a club or activity that has no meaning or impact will not result in personal growth or impress an admissions officer. I tell all students that no credit is given just for showing up or attending a lunchtime meeting. They must find a way to make a meaningful impact or difference.

College application essays encourage applicants to write about the impact that they made, not to list an organization's name or their position. Some students I have worked with who have been the most successful in the college application process have eschewed titles and focused strictly on finding their own way to grow and make a difference. Real-world experience and skill development trump affiliation with prestigious-sounding organizations or roles that offer no true responsibilities or opportunities to grow. This holds true especially for community service organizations. With so much unmet need in the world, admissions officers prefer to admit applicants who are able to make a tangible difference on their own or with smaller organizations rather than those who ride an organization's coattails but can't point to any accomplishments.

Talia, a mother deeply involved in several charitable organizations in her well-to-do community, was incredibly proud that her daughter belonged to a service organization that boasts thousands of members across the country. Membership requires both a parent and the child to join, and most chapters are located in equally well-to-do areas. Within my community, it is widely known as an organization that many parents join as a way to network. Members apply to join when their children are young, and the children are expected to stay involved until they graduate from high school. The commitment is impressive, but from a leadership development perspective, other opportunities can help young people learn how to make a more enduring impact more effectively.

The majority of the youth members receive titles in the organization, and Talia beamed as she listed the numerous different positions Jenny had held throughout her years of involvement. I asked Jenny to explain to me what she did in each of these roles, but it didn't seem like there was much to report.

When it came to the actual service component, many students prioritized participating in events that allowed the parents and students to mingle rather than actively help those in need. Jenny reported activities where students would make care packages or create cards for veterans or nurses. These are noble pursuits to show appreciation for others, but the direct impact on vulnerable or marginalized populations is light at best. I encouraged Jenny to find her own ways to make a tangible difference for people in need in her community, but Talia doubled down on her insistence that Jenny's roles would be more impressive than doing something on her own.

When the time came to apply to college, Jenny's first draft of her essay responding to how she made her community a better place touched upon her roles within the organization, the meetings she attended, and the cards she made for veterans, senior homes, and first responders. I asked her how these experiences improved her community, and her answer was that she was committed to the organization and that "I showed that I cared about other people."

While I applaud caring for others, I told Jenny and her mother that the experiences didn't demonstrate a tangible impact, especially compared to applicants who volunteered on their own without an organization—for example, at homeless shelters to babysit kids while their parents tried to get back on their feet or collecting bags of trash on the weekends to clean up local rivers or bays. I asked Talia and Jenny about which type of experience would be more persuasive, and Talia refused to acknowledge that her daughter, while boasting many titles, may not have made as big a difference as she could have had she spent her time more focused on impact rather than puffery. In the end, like Maggie, the applicant with the "perfect" resume, Jenny did not do as well as she would have hoped in her application process. Talia blamed the outcome on a bias against wealthy students applying to college. I wanted to tell her, but refrained from doing so, that the bias is against people who give lip service rather than true service to organizations in their communities.

This same concept also holds true when it comes time to pursue a career. I experienced it firsthand working in finance. I quit working at a lesser-known investment firm where I was doing a lot more substantive work to pursue a similar role at a much more "respected" firm. Everyone I knew talked about the deals the firm had done in the past, and it seemed like the perfect place for me to work and enhance my résumé and skill set. When I joined, I learned quickly that I had relied on the firm's past reputation. They had raised no capital to invest in new deals, and for months I alternated between twiddling my thumbs and pretending to run through the motions. While people were impressed when I told them that I worked there, I realized when I began interviewing at other companies that I had absolutely no growth opportunities as a finance professional to talk about. In each interview, I could only talk about my work experience from the less prestigious firm. In hindsight, I should have probably stayed at the less prestigious company because I would have developed more deal experience that would have helped me grow more. The fancy firm impressed outsiders, but I I ultimately fell victim to the puffery trap.

Between my students' experiences applying to college and my own work life, I have become a firm believer in the importance of real experiences and how much more valuable they are than the titles or names of the organizations that accompany them. At the end of the day, each person is evaluated based on their capabilities, not their titles or affiliations. A Harvard graduate who does not know how to write code will not be a more sought-after candidate for a job at a software company compared to someone who went to a junior college, transferred to a local four-year university, and is a skilled programmer.

A young person starting out on the journey to develop key life skills may need to start small to gain critical experience that allows them to close in on their ultimate goal. No one should view these experiences as beneath them. The focus should be on developing skills and perspective rather than acquiring titles or affiliations. When the right time comes, skills and perspectives can be applied to positions with titles and affiliations that are worthy of the time it took to develop them.

FINAL THOUGHTS ON LEADERSHIP

DEVELOPING INTO A LEADER IS A LIFELONG JOURNEY that rewards people for putting themselves out there to have new experiences, learn about themselves, and find a way to make an impact. Leadership comes in all shapes and sizes. It takes time for each person to find out what kind of leader they want to be and for what reasons they seek to lead. Aspiring leaders need to give themselves the time to find their path. Spreading oneself thin denies a person the chance to explore and commit to meaningful causes.

The type of leader a person grows into should be tailored to who they are, what they enjoy, and what they hope to accomplish. There isn't an objectively right leader to become. Instead, every young person should embrace the flexibility that being a leader provides them to find a way to make an impact that is meaningful and natural to them.

There is no need to follow the masses and do what everyone else is doing at school or elsewhere in the community. Everyone should play to their own unique strengths. This alone will allow each person to make a bigger impact—and the world needs all kinds of people.

Prioritize impact over title and affiliation. The skills we learn and the perspective we gain in pursuit of making a difference empower our future success, not empty titles on our résumés or our associations with impressive-sounding organizations. These acquired characteristics are transferable and what admissions officers and employers seek in applicants.

None of us has an exact grasp of where we are heading in life, but we have goals and dreams. Developing into an impactful leader can help each of us make the most of the journey and optimize the benefits of the end goal as well.

Part 3

PASSION

> I HAVE NO
> SPECIAL TALENTS.
> I AM ONLY PASSIONATELY
> CURIOUS.
>
> —ALBERT EINSTEIN

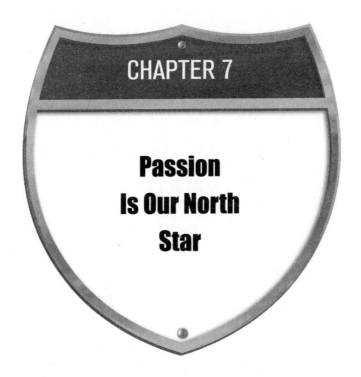

CHAPTER 7

Passion Is Our North Star

DEFINING TRAITS OF A PASSIONATE CHILD: *Exhibits a strong feeling of enthusiasm or excitement either for something that interests them or about doing something that speaks to them. Children with passion pursue a cause or activity because it excites them. As a result, they need no encouragement to dedicate themselves to that cause or activity. Passion is about emotions and what makes us feel good. This is different from purpose, which is the reason or the "why" behind what we do. There are no right or wrong passions. Passions are unique to each child*

and should be the child's and no one else's. While a parent can intro-
duce a child to a passion, true passion must come from within.

BEHAVIOR PATTERNS: *When we practice our passions, we can feel*
excited and hopeful rather than stressed and burdened. Pursuing one's
passions in the course of one's career can bring greater fulfillment from
the contributions made in the workplace.

WHEN I MEET STUDENTS FOR THE FIRST TIME, I always
ask, "Where do you see yourself in ten years?" The question isn't
the expected "Where do you want to go to college?" which, while
important, focuses on the short term and forces students to define
their progress within the bounds of their education thus far. Instead,
I want to know about their interests and future goals, because defining them helps give students direction, and direction is what any
successful young person needs.

Of course, direction is *also* key to guiding students to the best
college for them. And that process starts with one of the first steps
toward building a successful college application: picking high school
classes. I always instruct students to choose their classes and extracurriculars wisely, because a cohesive application theme that plays
to each student's strengths and interests is a hallmark of a successful
college application. For example, passion for math is what drives a
student to throw themselves into the throes of AP Calculus when the
rest of us would rather skip it for a class with an easy A waiting for us.
This is a good indicator that AP Calculus is the right choice for your
child, whereas a different student who enjoys reading and writing
might be better off taking AP English Literature or AP U.S. History
instead. (Best of all, a child who can identify their passion gives the
parent a break from one of the most unpleasant parts of parenting:

nagging! There is no need to nag a child who is passionate about doing a certain activity or a field of study. Passionate children will do whatever it takes to pursue their passions as far as they can go.)

Beyond the high school transcript, passion helps young people start to figure out their eventual career path and place in the world. Once in the working world, young people with passion go the extra distance when frustrated. No matter which career they choose, they will meet challenges and hardships that passion will better equip them to overcome. While passion in and of itself does not lead to success, it facilitates the type of behavior needed for someone to climb the ladder.

With passion, it's not about being the best or the most successful; it is more about mastering something that is meaningful, inspiring, and engaging. The excitement that passion provides leads to the drive that ultimately results in success. In a study from the Norwegian University of Science and Technology on the most talented soccer players seeking to make the national developmental team, researchers found that the players who reported the strongest passion for the sport in written questionnaires performed the best on the field. Researchers were able to isolate passion from grit and a positive mindset as a stand-alone factor for performance.[21] Thus, proof exists that when people love what they dedicate themselves to, they do better at that pursuit. This underscores the need for each of us to commit ourselves to what inspires and excites us.

We seek to tap into others' passion and are drawn to passionate leaders' orbits because their passion is contagious. Leaders who are passionate about and committed to their causes go the extra distance to ensure that those they lead are able to execute their vision as well. Simply, passion is infectious. More importantly, passion empowers those who possess it to deploy their grit to stay the course, despite how challenging it may be. Passion also calls on leaders to find ways to be effective in their roles.

Passion is important for each of us, but it doesn't necessarily just fall into our laps. It requires effort to identify. In an era when it is easy to stay at home all day and not fully engage with the world, parents must be intentional with helping their children find a passion beyond video games, social media, or hanging out with their friends—something based on what they enjoy or find interesting. As the village that it takes to raise a child, we need to lead with passion rather than outcomes. Passion keeps children engaged and growing, allowing them to change course if and when that is needed.

Our passions evolve, which is perfectly fine. Passions need at a certain point to be rooted in the practical world with which we interact. A passion for video games is fine for a child. But when approaching adulthood, that passion needs to be channeled into something that allows an adult to thrive independently. I constantly tell students that they will find success when they identify the intersection of what they love, what they are good at, and where an opportunity arises to apply those loves and skills.

A friend from high school who loved to bake and also had an incredible knack for social media was able to build a multimillion-dollar cookie business. Prior to launching her passion project on the side of her marketing job, she bounced from position to position. Her positions looked good on paper and tapped into what was likely expected of her in the community. But where was it actually leading her? When she dedicated herself to baking, at which she excelled, she found success. Not every baker can create a successful cookie company, but this particular person would not have found her own success had she not committed herself to doing what she was good at and loved.

Passion discovery can seem challenging and sometimes can box a young person in and make them uncomfortable trying to define their future. Long pauses often follow these seemingly obvious questions:

"What do you want to be when you grow up?"

"Where do you want to go to college?"

"What do you want to study in college?"

These questions are not easy for a young person to answer. From my experience, they often cause young people to shut down and answer with "I don't know." Yes, these questions speak to what interests a person, but they are based on the assumption that a young person already knows what they want in life. It's normal to not have it all figured out, especially at a young age. And if we are being honest, many young people's parents themselves are still trying to figure out what *they* want to do while their kids are being asked the same question. If anything, not having all the answers gives young people the chance to explore new opportunities and find what is a great fit for them.

Rather than asking for commitment to a path that is based on a specific career or educational plan, we can take the pressure off young people by encouraging them to discover and then later dedicate themselves to their passions. Ask them these three questions that put passion at the center of the journey:

1. What do you enjoy?

Discovering what we truly enjoy is a lot harder than it sounds. Just as we have to work hard at our passions, we have to put in the work to try new things for ourselves to see if we are willing to work at them. In the media age, too many students think they want to pursue a certain career because it looks good on TV. Unfortunately, being a doctor or lawyer may be much less romantic than *Grey's Anatomy* or *Suits* makes it out to be.

Parents should aim their children toward experiences and careers that they enjoy because it will be more effective for their future well-being rather than simply pushing them toward a career purely for the sake of financial stability. While nothing is wrong with wanting financially secure lives, we also need to take students' passions into account. We set our kids up for a very challenging life if we push them to pursue careers *purely* for the purpose of material comfort. Parents are critical to this process as they are the biggest source of guidance for career planning with their young adult children. Forty-eight percent of recent Gen Z college graduates reported being influenced by their parents when choosing a career path.[22] But by taking passion into account, parents can succeed at both: We help our kids reach fulfillment and enjoy themselves, and that enjoyment and desire for fulfillment will, in turn, help them better reach financial success because they will be more driven and willing to work.

The journey to discovering what a person enjoys should occur early in their education. As young people move through middle and high school, they have opportunities to explore and develop their interests. Tie high school courses and extracurricular activities to passion development, not to building up an artificial résumé that is designed to impress admissions officers. Students with an interest in STEM (science, technology, engineering, and mathematics) fields can see for themselves if they like the analytical math and science frameworks that the subjects are built around by taking more advanced classes that their schools offer. Students interested in the humanities or social sciences can avail themselves of more rigorous history, English, and world language classes. Regardless of a student's interests, look to local community colleges for summer courses that can introduce them to practical fields like business, engineering, the law, and public health. These courses can be included in a college application and enhance an applicant's transcript. But far more important than any boost to their GPA and résumés, these courses can introduce young people to fields they may not have exposure to in school so they can see what motivates them.

Extracurricular activities are also a great hands-on way to see what young people enjoy. Students who think they may be interested in engineering could join their high school's robotics team and gauge for themselves if they enjoy building and programming autonomous robots. Use the experience to determine a course of action. A student who has no interest in joining the robotics team at their school has a pretty good indicator that the field may not be for them later in life either. A student with an interest in the law could join mock trial, while a young person who is the peacemaker for their friends at school or their siblings at home could apply their talents to Model United Nations. Even if they do not want to become a diplomat, students could develop their debating skills, which can be applied to a myriad of other pursuits. Conversely, an aspiring law student who joins mock trial and hates it will know that a legal career might not be the best path forward, which might save them a lot of disappointment or frustration later.

Leaning into interests and pursuing activities they enjoy teaches young people to be intentional with their time and prioritize their interests. While we are each required to do things we don't enjoy (studying for a college entrance exam is one that comes to mind for a teenager), we should enjoy the overall path each of us is on. We're lucky to live in a society in which the diversity of career opportunities is great, and there are many paths to financial independence—something parents at a minimum want for their children—that lie outside the traditional realm of doctor, lawyer, and engineer.

With so many opportunities and a society that celebrates innovating one's own career, why should we force a young person to pursue jobs that match neither their aptitude nor attitude? Individuals who don't enjoy writing will not enjoy the practice of law. People who don't enjoy being analytical may not enjoy being an engineer. But a person who enjoys learning about how the body works and interacting with others may love being a healthcare provider and find meaning and purpose in the extended education and paperwork that accompany treating patients. A sense of enjoyment makes the unpleasant parts of our daily lives and careers worth it and serves as a reminder of why we are on our specific individual paths.

I did not enjoy creating financial models as an investment banker out of college. I found it difficult to tolerate the very long hours and mundane tasks that also accompanied my job. Every part of the job actually set me off because I didn't enjoy the key parts of it. I made silly mistakes in my work because my heart wasn't in it, and my managers constantly called me out for my lack of attention to detail. But the underlying issue was how little I cared about the job, which showed in my performance. Even though banking is traditionally a lucrative career path, I had trouble doing a good job and would have struggled to advance my career because of how much I disliked it. It took courage to walk away from it and an open mind to try something new, but walking away from banking allowed me to try something new that led me to find my passion.

When I started counseling young people, I discovered that I really loved what I did. I didn't mind waking up early to get to work or taking calls late at night from stressed-out students or their parents. My enjoyment led me to throw myself into my pursuit, which empowered me to perform much more strongly than I did as a banker. I would receive feedback from parents telling me they could see how much I cared and how they felt good working with me. In short, enjoying what I was doing was a key factor in my growth as a college admissions adviser. I wish for my students nothing more than to enjoy how they spend their time because this will lead to their future success.

Prioritize your child's enjoyment and help them find ways to grow through it. A young person who enjoys building things may love being an engineer. Someone who enjoys traveling may love becoming a pilot and being paid to take people to new places. Incredible opportunities accompany every interest; it just requires each of us to be honest with what we enjoy and make a game plan based on that.

2. What are you good at?

Many people love doing things that they are good at, but there is a key difference between enjoying something and excelling at it. I have worked with students who find medicine interesting but are deeply uncomfortable around blood. It is perfectly fine if they are not meant to go to medical school because their anxiety around aspects of human health prevents them from being effective healthcare providers. Young people should play to their strengths, giving them the highest possible odds for success in an increasingly competitive world. We need to be honest with ourselves about what we excel at and pursue growth opportunities based on those skills rather than conforming to other paths that are not suited to who we are. Instead of comparing the nature of one's pursuits to those of others around us, each young person should find a pursuit they enjoy and can excel in, and then constantly strive to better themselves. Even with passion, every successful career requires work. It's therefore paramount to at least enjoy or take satisfaction in what we choose to pursue. Otherwise, we sign ourselves up for a lifetime of struggle.

Countless students tell me they want to be programmers because of all the news coverage of young and successful tech entrepreneurs making fortunes launching software products. But when these students dislike coding, I encourage them to pursue other dreams. Yes, there are incredible opportunities for programmers to do well financially, but succeeding requires an ability to code in a way that creates enormous value. While coding can be learned, equally successful people focus on what they are good at. Just because Silicon Valley gets a lot of media airtime doesn't mean it's the only path to financial success.

Each of us must be honest about our strengths and weaknesses. Such honesty and self-examination requires actually analyzing what a path requires of the person pursuing it. Ask people who have achieved their career goal what their work entails on a daily basis. Many parents tell me their children would make great lawyers because they are skilled arguers but fail to take into consideration that practicing law also requires attorneys to read and write well, which may not be their children's core skills.

Many people are enticed by fancy labels and intimidated by the strengths of their peers. Comparing our strengths to others' is not necessary. We may be good at math, and others are likely even better than we are. That doesn't mean we should shy away from an analytical field. Our strengths are unique to us. We simply need to be honest as to what those strengths are to ensure that the steps we take in life reflect who we are. Ask yourself: *If money and prestige weren't issues, what would I want to pursue?*

Not all of us know our strengths, and that's perfectly normal. Believe it or not, determining your strengths and passions can require work too. (Hard work: you can't escape it!) Until we seriously try things for ourselves, we have no way of knowing what we are good at and what we like. For example, I insist that every student interested in becoming a software programmer try taking a computer science class at their high school or local community college not only to see if they enjoy the material but also if the skills and concepts come naturally to them. Everyone gets excited about building the next big app, but actually doing so requires a lot of work, patience, and skill.

Very few people enjoy the challenge of swimming upstream—and none of us should need to. Many careers get a lot of hype in the media, but they are not the only way to earn a living. Students who dislike math and computers shouldn't be forced to pursue programming. Would-be programmers need to understand the task for what it is, and not just look at the *Forbes* cover stories. The same goes for traditionally prestigious careers like investment banking, law, and medicine. Only those who are well suited for these careers will make successful bankers, lawyers, and doctors. If you have zero interest in finance, no amount of media prestige will make you happy.

Plenty of other careers may receive less media coverage or discussion time around the dinner table but bring financial security and a better fit for those who pursue them. The important thing is

staying true to what we excel at and who we are, which can sometimes be challenging under immense peer and familial pressure. A
friend from college, John, studied finance because we were students
at Wharton and there was immense peer pressure to pursue the most
sought-after major there. After graduating, he decided to work in
financial planning at Google because it seemed like the right thing
to do with a finance degree. After all, it was a growing company that
was redefining the Information Age. But John was a creative at heart
and was constantly sending out renderings of buildings he saw that
he thought could be redeveloped into something bigger and better.
The feedback John received during the course of his early career focused consistently on room for improvement in his financial mod-
eling skills. His managers expected him to keep growing, and while
he did to a certain extent, he was not keeping up with other analysts
at the same career level.

While it took John much courage to leave such a sought-after position, he eventually applied to an architecture program for graduate
school. Many naysayers said that he was foolish for walking away
from a career at Google for something that was so speculative. What
those people did not realize was that he may not have had much
of a career at Google because the skills they needed in his position
didn't align with who he was as a person and what he was capable
of achieving. John thrived in his architecture program and ended up
working for a prominent architect before starting his own studio. He
is far more successful as an architect than he likely would have been
had he remained with the tech giant. Yes, some people earn millions
in stock options from tech companies, but they have to earn it. Who
knows if John had the skills to do that? It isn't worth finding out,

because he discovered his path to success by focusing on what he actually excelled at: design.

Every young person must possess the inner strength and confidence to chase their passions like John did, especially if they are in nontraditional fields. Many people are deterred because the negative feedback they receive from their community can fill them with doubt. When it comes to college admission, many colleges ask students to write about why they want to study in their intended field. This question is designed to measure passion, and genuine answers that speak to specific experiences a student had to foster that passion tend to outperform insincere essays or explanations that lack a real justification.

The Internet offers a variety of strength and skill assessments. While software cannot tell us what we are good at, it can prompt us through targeted questions to reflect on our skills. Parents can sometimes see things in their children that are harder for them to see in themselves. Parents should have questions that lean into the strengths they see in their child and encourage them to see it in themselves based on these observations.

Playing to one's strengths also helps with college admission, graduate school, and even building a strong transcript for the first job out of college because it gives a student the opportunity to pick classes and fields that play to their strengths and ensure academic success. With many selective public and private universities setting high academic standards for admission, applicants can afford a few hiccups on their transcript and remain competitive. Math-oriented students can focus on taking advanced math classes and not feel the pressure to take advanced social studies or humanities classes. Admissions officers will focus on their achievements in the math field and weigh them much more heavily than in less relevant fields for their intended path. Even with entry-level jobs, hiring managers rely on college coursework for assessing preparation for the job and focus on the subjects that are relevant to their fields as well.

3. Where do these opportunities exist in the world?

Each of us has to balance our strengths and interests with the realities of the world and how it is changing. While many more career opportunities exist in the modern age, especially with the advent of more advanced technology, some industries, while accessible, are still much harder to break into. For example, young people who love film may read into questions one and two and see their path to pursuing film as a career. Yes, there are directors, actors, and film producers who are able to financially support themselves by dedicating themselves to their careers. But for every Steven Spielberg or Jennifer Lawrence, countless directors, writers, and actors are not able to support themselves financially despite their talents and passions.

We need to be honest with ourselves about what opportunities exist for our passions and find ways to be flexible with them to achieve our long-term goals. Are we okay with the risk that the most probable outcome for a person who wants to become an actor is to struggle for years financially without ever getting the big break? Are we willing to put in the hard work to turn our passions into reality because passion alone will not carry the day for any of us? If the answer is yes to these questions, make an informed decision.

Luckily, thanks to new types of careers that grow in relevance every day, many career options are available for someone of any strength. People who enjoy creating can pursue careers in anything from marketing and public relations to app building and online community building. These are all wildly different career paths in vastly different industries that look for people with unique sets of skills but who all share the same passion for creation.

Young people today need to be open-minded and flexible when it comes to assessing opportunities for them to grow. The most promising fields for tomorrow may not currently exist. Labor markets and career paths are poised for seismic changes as artificial intelligence replaces many routine and even analytical tasks that professionals currently perform. With so much uncertainty in the world and concern about what the future may hold, young people today should embrace flexibility so they can pursue new opportunities that are relevant to who they are and fit with the coming changes.

Beyond a flexible mindset, a young person should be intentional in incorporating their education into the answers to these three preceding questions. What skills should they acquire to be proficient at what they want to do? What experiences should they gain along the way to prepare themselves for their paths? How can they expose themselves to different opportunities to find what they enjoy and are good at doing? Who should they meet and what should they study to assess where the opportunities lie in their paths? This could mean prioritizing colleges that offer internships or project-based learning or are located in places with opportunities to network and gain exposure to specific fields or relevant industries. The questions *not* posed include "Is [fancy-named school] good enough?" or "Will this university open up doors for me?" Prestige does not lead to success or fulfillment, and no student will get everything out of college that they deserve unless they have direction on how a college education can help them achieve their goals.

While it can take a lifetime to develop answers to these questions, colleges can help students do that if they offer opportunities for students to engage in the world around them. For the "I don't know" student, prioritize colleges that offer opportunities to explore beyond the classroom and be intentional with finding paths that are guided by passion, exploration, and development.

Fulfillment lies at the intersection of the answers to these three primary questions about passion. A person can be passionate and great at something they love doing, but they also need to ensure that they can support themselves. With passion, a young person can determine what they need to do to grow into who they want to become and what they want to do. The steps to be taken, skills to be acquired, and perspective to be gained will flow naturally, decreasing the stress and pressure a teenager feels to have it all figured out. The world may be very different ten years from now. Students who know their passion can grow and be prepared to make the most of the changing world they will inherit.

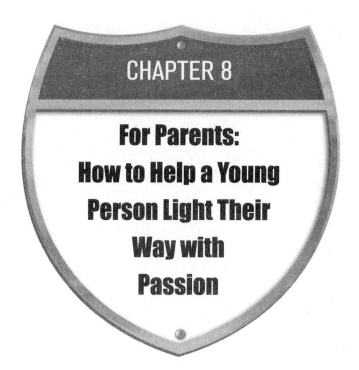

CHAPTER 8

For Parents: How to Help a Young Person Light Their Way with Passion

IN THE INFORMATION AGE, we can explore anything and everything at once, but immense information overload can sometimes make it harder to take the first step in forging a path to action. Even once we find that path, it's easy for the oversharing around us to be distracting—and make it difficult to stay on a single path and keep developing. Honing in on a truly enjoyable and fulfilling passion helps keep young people focused, engaged, and reflective.

Passions come from within a person. As a parent, you can only prod and guide so much. Students ultimately need space to discover their own passions to ensure that they are willing to invest time in pursuing them. Leading with passion at the forefront of their development can help ensure that a young person dedicates themselves to what is actually meaningful to them and avoid pursuing a bunch of meaningless activities about which they feel only a mediocre interest. Parents should heed the following advice.

DO: Prioritize their long-term fulfillment over short-term prestige.

We often mistake the excitement that comes with owning covetable labels for the excitement that accompanies true passion. It's easy to be distracted. On the journey of life, many shiny labels, high-profile university nameplates, and fancy-sounding jobs seem attractive but actually distract us from our ultimate goals because they are not a good fit.

Yet many people are swept up in the excitement and buzz that comes with these exciting labels, and they mistake that buzz for passion. (It's also easy to read a book like this and think, *But I don't do that!* Trust me, we all do this to an extent.) The people who can't be honest with themselves, however, then devote their careers and lives to pursuing activities simply because they sound good on a résumé.

This happens often with college, as one can imagine. Parents may aspire for their kids to attend prestigious universities because they believe it will set up their students for long-term success. We may dream of our teens becoming doctors or other learned professionals who make an impact on others' lives while achieving financial stability. But how can we tell the difference between someone who is truly passionate about medicine and public health and a family who thinks premed at Stanford will sound impressive to potential dates or friends at cocktail parties? There's a fine line between chasing a label because it aligns with our passions and goals and doing it because it sounds good.

Being distracted by short-term prestige is incredibly easy because at first glance it may seem like attending a fancy university or pursuing an enviable career path will lead to fulfillment. And if we are being honest, most people like the sound of their offspring graduating from a place like Harvard or having an MD behind their name. However, parents need to be honest with themselves and how they weigh short-term achievements with the path to long-term fulfillment, because they may not be the same.

Prioritizing prestige takes the focus away from the child and places it on some standard that is meant to impress others rather than addressing the core of what will make a person happy and fulfilled. We need to be aware of the dark side of prestige-focused parenting: What happens when the obsession with prestige, perfection, and obtaining something incredibly difficult backfires? What about when kids burn out, become depressed, or snap? These questions are particularly relevant given the fact that the label associated with a college degree does not guarantee or even necessarily bring a student closer to their goals. Graduating from Harvard or any other name-brand school does not ensure that a student will be able to use their degree in a way that helps them achieve success. Unfortunately, these concerns are incredibly common, particularly in communities that value appearances over developing a foundation for long-term fulfillment.

I once worked with a student, Brian, who was passionate about computer science. With his goals in mind, Brian gained admission to and enrolled at Santa Clara University in San Jose, which has one of the strongest pipelines for graduates interested in working as software programmers. While it's not an Ivy, it's a well-respected university with a prime location and many benefits. Many of the faculty at this university have industry experience and connections. The proximity to Silicon Valley allows for incredible networking and internship opportunities for students to pursue their dreams. But despite the fact that Brian excelled academically and made friends, his mother, Judy, insisted that he transfer to a more prestigious university on the East Coast that "had higher national rankings in case her son wanted to pursue a different career."

Well, he didn't. He loved his classes and wanted to stay put and continue on the path that would help him establish a career in computer science, his passion. Despite his best efforts, Brian's mom still insisted that it was good practice to apply to other colleges because transferring to another university could never hurt. While perhaps true on its face, Judy missed the point. Yes, having options at any stage of life is wonderful, but at a certain point, life does in fact reward those who commit, whether to an education or career path, relationships, or other aspects of life. After all, we can only really hone in and perfect our craft once we've decided on one.

Given that Brian was happy and building a foundation for his life, and rather than distract him from his goals and contentment, Judy should have encouraged her son to seek out networking opportunities and develop additional skills that would enhance his education and subsequent steps in life. Instead, she was so concerned about the need for Brian to attend a college with a fancy "label"—like an Ivy—that she insisted he spend time on transfer applications instead of internship applications. Naturally, when Brian failed to obtain a software engineering internship, he was incredibly frustrated—because of his mom's unreasonable demands. When he was not hired for a summer internship, Judy renewed her calls for him to transfer and used his lack of an internship as justification for why he needed to leave for a "better" school. How can you even argue with that?

From a reader's perspective, Judy may sound nuts and completely off-kilter. But really, she meant well and is fairly typical of parents in high-income communities. Unfortunately, the reality is that we are becoming more caught up in the endless pursuit of prestigious labels, which has engendered a culture where winning—however we define that—is more important than where the result leads. For some hyper-competitive, prestige-focused parents, it is more important that their children outperform their peers in any given aspect rather than find and develop their own path and passion.

I have yet to meet a Stanford-or-bust parent convinced that they are raising the next Mark Zuckerberg who will agree to let their child apply to San Jose State University. What they don't realize is that San Jose State is located in the heart of Silicon Valley and boasts more graduates working in sought-after tech companies than any other university in the nation. It beat out both Harvard and the University of Pennsylvania's Wharton School of Business in terms of the number of alumni working at Fortune 500 companies.

The most poignant example of suffering at the hands of prestige is shown through statistics about law school students. A law degree and profession are traditionally regarded as a path to a high-earning and prestigious career, which is why many families push their children to become lawyers. However, only 10 percent of law school graduates reported being offered positions at law firms with more than 250 lawyers—the firms that pay salaries of close to $200,000 for new attorneys. For the remainder of law school graduates—the

90 percent who are unable to land a position at a large law firm—the average salary is $52,329.

Given the odds and what practicing law entails for most incoming lawyers, we must ask ourselves: Is the legal education worth it? Is it a fit for my child? Is it worth the cost? If the answer is no, then is it worth inflating our own egos to brag that our child is going to law school if it is setting them up for likely financial struggles and high levels of stress? The irony is that if students pursue a career like law simply for prestige, they may end up with jobs that do not cover their living expenses and student loans.

When it comes to the actual value of prestige, I think back to when I found out that the barista at my Starbucks who made my coffee every morning was exactly my age and a Duke grad. I was shocked to learn that she had little to no other prospective job options. Armed with a fancy degree in a major with few career opportunities, she was adrift, floundering, and underemployed. Clearly, this high-end label of a degree was not enough to build a life.

With higher education, we must embrace that an education is a means to an end, not the be-all and end-all. The cost of the education determines our return on an investment. Going to a prestigious private university is a fantastic accomplishment, but if it saddles a young adult with $300,000 of student loans and prohibits them from becoming financially independent and achieving key life milestones, then is it worth it?

Prioritize the long-term path over short-term prestige. This will allow a young person to identify the myriad ways they can prepare themselves for their bright futures through their education. It also forces the student to think critically about key aspects of their education and career path rather than just the university's name value.

Take, for example, an Ivy League school like Dartmouth. While prestigious, its rural New Hampshire location is arguably not the best fit for many students who are seeking internships in, say, the financial sector. Those students will probably be better off focusing on applying to a school like New York University, which, while not an Ivy, is located in downtown Manhattan, not far from the financial district.

When considering the long-term path, two things can help: seeking meaningful internships and quality mentors. Meaningful internships give your student a glimpse into what it's really like to work in an industry, which is crucial to deciding on their future career path. Law, for example, may sound exciting to them when they're debating the constitutionality of the Electoral College in class, but consistently pulling late nights at the law office may be an entirely different experience. Only by interning at a law firm and learning how it operates will they be able to tell if law is their proper career path.

Quality mentors can help guide your student on their path by giving them experience opportunities, guiding them through school and networking, and putting them in touch with the mentor's colleagues to allow them to diversify their internship and educational experience.

Many schools place a big emphasis on mentorships and internships, which adds to their appeal. Part of the reason the Honors Colleges at the University of Arizona and Arizona State University produce more Rhodes and Fulbright Scholars than the entire Ivy League put together is that the academic communities there are committed to your student's long-term success. They flag opportunities that may enhance your child's education and prepare them for the future. Careers and industries are rapidly evolving, and parents aren't always the best equipped to help their children—especially if they are unfamiliar with their kids' long-term paths and the workforce of the future. Embrace the fact that, as a parent, you may be best playing a secondary role and seek out others who can provide appropriate guidance and support. Empower your child to look beyond their immediate network and contact others through college networks, LinkedIn, and the larger communities to which they belong. With so much uncertainty about the future, having a plan and a desire to seek help from those best positioned to navigate the future can make the path ahead more rewarding and enjoyable.

DO: Promote a healthy relationship with sports.

Sports feels like it should be its own category with respect to passion because the most frequent question I am asked is whether students must play a sport to earn admission to their dream college. In a sports culture that glorifies the idea that anyone can become a superstar, it's tempting to try to become one. But while we can—and often are—passionate about sports, both professional and youth, the odds are heavily stacked against success on this path. Even if parents prioritize athletic achievement, they should still encourage their children to develop passions outside sports.

Students *absolutely do not* need to play a sport to earn admission to their dream college. Colleges are, after all, first and foremost *academic*, not athletic, institutions. In fact, collegiate athletic statistics will shock you. Out of all the students who think they have a shot at playing in college and going pro, only a measly 6 percent of high school athletes are recruited to play at the intercollegiate varsity level (and just one-third of those, or 2 percent of all high school athletes, receive athletic scholarships). Regardless of athletic ability, statistically speaking, a high school athlete has significantly higher odds of earning a merit scholarship for academic performance.

Here's the reasoning behind the athletic value proposition equation: When college admissions officers are deciding who to admit to their university, they are evaluating an applicant's ability to add to their school's community. For some lucky athletes who happen to be at the right skill level at a time when coaches are looking to fill a particular position on a team, those students are able to leverage their athletic ability in addition to their academic ability and earn admission to universities whose teams can use their sports skills.

But this concept—universities looking for students with the potential to contribute to their campus—holds true for *all* prospective students. Colleges are seeking out students with the potential to contribute academically through research, land internships at local companies, start nonprofits to uplift the surrounding community, and, yes, fill out their athletic teams. In every field, admissions officers are assessing whether students will contribute on campus. Sports is just one of these fields. Unless a student is specifically recruited to play on a college sports team, athletic ability is not a factor for college admission. Admissions officers do not care about performance in high school or club sports if there is no college recruitment potential. The most a high school athletic career will do for an applicant is demonstrate their ability to lead a team or have the discipline to practice daily.

Athletic recruitment, specifically, is so rare because seldom does a specific student's athletic ability align with a college team's needs. A student swimmer may be an incredible sprint freestyler and aspire to perform at Duke. However, if, in their application year, Duke already has a full roster of freestyle swimmers, the Blue Devils coach will not even be looking to recruit a freestyle swimmer, no matter how talented. And even if there are open spots on teams, athletes from all over the world will be competing for one or two places. Of course, it's important to keep an open mind should an athletic recruitment opportunity come your way. But with such low odds, why pin all your college hopes on something that may or may not work out? Rather, we should take a balanced approach toward sports. Don't let your student's academics slip because they think they can rely on athletic recruitment.

On the financial front, many families also disregard tuition planning because they think that their student-athlete will earn a lucrative athletic scholarship. Here's an athletic scholarship phenomenon for you: Many colleges don't offer athletic scholarships at all. For example, Harvard and all the other Ivy League universities do not offer merit-based athletic scholarships under any circumstances. Given this additional hurdle, while investing in athletic development is a worthy expense and has many health and lifestyle benefits, athletics should not be the *only* thing that students rely on to carry them through the college application process.

The reality is that, unless you are a professional athlete (which, again, only a minuscule percentage of the population achieves), life rewards you more for exhibiting applicable skills that you pick up in the classroom, internships, or club leadership positions. For us normal people who are not destined to be professional athletes, we should play sports to the extent that it can enrich our lives with healthy movement and teach us the discipline needed to practice and get through a difficult workout. But sports should not crowd out other activities like academics, job opportunities, community service, and extracurriculars. Eighty percent of kids enrolled in youth sports quit by age fifteen due to the disparity between the kid wanting to have fun and the parent wanting to win at all costs.[23]

Take the example of Jim. I began working with Jim's high school–age students as they approached the application process. With the older two boys, sports achievement followed academic achievement as they were able to balance straight As with sports practices and games.

However, the youngest, Robby, had a learning difference and needed to spend extra time on homework and practicing what was covered in class to build his academic foundation. Robby struggled with basic reading and math, and it was painful for his self-esteem. To build up his son's confidence, Jim began telling Robby that it was "okay to not be good at reading or writing" and that he "could go play catch outside" after school instead because he had great potential as an athlete.

News flash: Regardless of how great an athlete one's child is, the reading and writing part of the young person's life isn't going anywhere. While Robby doesn't need to be the next Mark Twain, he does need to spend time becoming proficient in the core academic skills to build a foundation for everything that comes outside the sports arena—including his education and career. Jim was effectively putting all Robby's future eggs in the sports basket, which we now know is a statistically irrational decision. Perhaps the extra time would have been better spent practicing grammar and writing skills so that Robby could catch up to his peers. And while I want every child to have as much fun as possible and to be confident, more importantly

I want Robby to be positioned to achieve all his goals throughout his entire life. Sports can only take someone so far.

As Robby grew throughout high school, it became clear that despite his best efforts, he was not developing into an elite potential college athlete. While pursuing his sport with all his being, he also did not build the academic foundation to directly attend a four-year university after graduating from high school and will enroll in a community college when he graduates.

No matter the consequences with their academic or personal growth, an obsession with sports can change a child's path to maturity as well. Growing up, my brother and I were often put on the same teams with a kid from our school, Tim, who was on the shorter side. He tried valiantly with basketball but struggled to stand out as an athlete since the sport rewarded being bigger and stronger. When he discovered golf, it seemed like a natural fit and he emerged quickly as a good, but not great, player.

As high school approached, Tim's parents, knowing that the local public high school had the best golf team in the state, decided to hold him back and repeat eighth grade, claiming that he had been diagnosed with a "learning disorder." A B student, Tim's academic performance was average. But rather than risk not making the golf team, Tim repeated eighth grade and began practicing golf every day for five hours a day.

Flash forward fifteen years: Every decision Tim made has revolved around golf. With golf as his only forte, his only recruitment offer came from a small and relatively unknown college. When he graduated and was confronted with the reality that he was not a professional-level golfer, he nonetheless moved to South Africa to chase his dream on a minor pro tour. While money isn't everything, in his first several seasons, Tim averaged $30,000 per year in winnings, which were dwarfed by his travel costs and tournament fees. When he finally flamed out of the qualifying tour, he relocated to Canada, where he now teaches golf lessons in a community where, due to weather, the golf season lasts five months of the year. While chasing one's dream is admirable, in the case of this golfer, Tim never had the chance to even form or entertain any other dreams or pursuits that may have allowed him to develop skills or perspectives for life outside of golf, which would likely come in handy. I cannot help but wonder what else he could have done had he simply been encouraged to focus on anything in addition to golf throughout his upbringing.

Even though these stories are common, I still meet with countless students who are passionate about playing their sport and fully committed to it. However, when I ask them what they want to do when they grow up, the question makes them uncomfortable. Here's a snippet of a conversation I had during an initial planning meeting with Eric, whose only extracurricular activity was playing water polo:

Me: So, beyond college, what do you see yourself doing in ten years?

Eric: In ten years? Um. *[pauses]* What do you mean, sorry?

Me: What do you want to be when you grow up? What kind of career do you see yourself having, and what kind of life do you envision yourself living? Any long-term goals and dreams? *[long pause]* And if you don't know, that's totally okay!

Eric: Yeah, I'm not really sure.

Me: Okay! So, besides water polo, what else do you like to do?

Eric: Well, water polo is pretty busy with games and practices, and when I'm not doing that I'm usually just doing homework. It's really busy, and it's hard to find time for anything else.

While life shouldn't be either just about making future plans or living in the moment, Eric has clearly blinded himself to the real world that awaits him. Without spending any time considering life after youth sports, he is depriving himself of the chance to prepare for his path when he discovers what it is. Studies on the development of elite high school athletes suggest that this problem is widespread. For example, in analyzing the career and life readiness of high school athletes in Kansas, researchers found that while sports can provide enough direction through goal setting and discipline in high school, challenges arise when these students face the cold reality that outside of professional sports, the world prioritizes nonathletic achievement. Students who place athletics before academics have substantially lower GPAs, attend class less frequently, are less prepared for life after high school, are less likely to graduate from college, and are more likely to mistakenly believe pro sports are in their future.[24]

When it comes to sports, like all other aspects of life, we must strive to ensure that young people have the balance to grow and develop in ways that are critical to their long-term fulfillment. In Robby's case, it means setting aside time for academic development. With Tim and Eric, this should include exploring life beyond the golf course or pool. Sports provide a positive feedback loop that comes from performing well in games or events. Parents must strive to provide structure and direction outside of athletics to ensure that students feel a sense of purpose and direction beyond the playing arena. Set aside time for everything else that matters, and validate aspects of one's identity that extend beyond sports. We need to celebrate young people for being thoughtful, creative, artistic, and engaged in their communities as much as we celebrate them for being elite-level athletes.

If athletics during the school year leave little time for other pursuits, that is okay. Double down on service and other growth opportunities in the summer, during school breaks, and when the sport is not in season. It is hard to balance so many competing interests and commitments, but the balancing act of life requires us to do this as young people and well into adulthood.

Parents can frame the decision for their kids with some simple questions: How should they invest their time? Do they need to study for a test? If so, for how much time? Does a sports practice conflict with that? How can both happen? Does the student need to study extra on the weekend? Is there something they can miss or reschedule? Identify what the priorities are at any given point in time and chase them.

Do not neglect probing conversations about life after sports either. There may not be a lot of time during the sports season for exploring outside passions, but community college classes can expose young people to different career paths along with informational conversations with professionals who can share their life experiences. Integrating passion development with athletic commitments will look different for each athlete. The key is to set aside time to ensure that the development occurs in conjunction with everything that sports have to offer young people.

DON'T: Make your child's life revolve around trophy collecting.

Passion is so important because it empowers us to dedicate ourselves to a real cause or activity that will allow us to benefit and give back to our society through our work, whatever that may be. It gives us a meaningful purpose that in turn enables us to keep going in the face of adversity. Passions need to be genuine. But sometimes people make their passion about constantly comparing and competing with people around them instead of focusing inward; this approach can lead to burnout, anxiety, and a lack of fulfillment.

For some, what they accomplish is less important than how the accomplishments measure up compared to others' achievements. The brand they seek is to be better than all the rest. Some parents are driven by the desire to see their child positioned as far superior to all others, even if it is unrealistic. With education, this means seeing their child attend Harvard or Stanford for no reason other than its high ranking and recognizable name. I refer to this behavior as *trophy collecting*.

Trophies designate performance relative to others competing for the same prize. They do not take into account luck, the journey to obtain them, or whether the recipient derives any fulfillment from them. A trophy is simply a measure of performance, and sometimes getting one can be nothing more than a Pyrrhic victory. Passion speaks to excitement from participating in an activity or pursuing a cause that is meaningful to an individual. It applies to topics of study, activities, careers, and how we spend our time. Passion is inconsistent with trophy collecting, which replaces genuine interest and excitement with a desire to have something out of reach for others. I worry for any child who is conditioned to simply achieve what the majority of others cannot and wonder about what happens when they fall short in their conquests or run out of trophies to collect.

Achievement for its own sake has a potentially toxic effect on those pursuing it. Admission to an Ivy League university requires close to perfect grades and test scores. It is estimated that over

45 percent of private high school students in the United States suffer from chronic anxiety as it relates to college admission.[25] While some stress is normal, is chronic anxiety in high school really worth it when we consider how subjective and arbitrary the modern college admissions process seems? Applicants can do everything right and still not earn admission to their dream college. Moreover, when students put so much pressure on themselves to rack up accolades and labels, they are learning that fulfillment comes from status rather than what inspires them and makes them happy.

The long-term adverse effects on a young person focused on trophy collecting for the sake of racking up awards was displayed by Taylor, whose especially distraught parents hired me after she was rejected from a summer program for high school students. Notably this camp was offered at Harvard, which is why they were especially disturbed.

Now, before I proceed any further with this story, I should mention that except for a few research-focused programs for high school students that are low cost or offer significant financial aid, being admitted to and participating in summer programs offered at colleges does not help students earn admission to highly selective schools. The reason is that the bulk of these programs are incredibly expensive and therefore not accessible to everyone who may apply to college.

Furthermore, organizations rent space and pay for the right to use the college's name in conjunction with the program, but the colleges themselves often have nothing to do with the program. Therefore, college admissions officers do not look favorably at camp participation. So when families ask me if these camps are worth it, I always let them know that's the case only if their child has a meaningful and valuable experience. The name of the camp alone doesn't matter for college admissions, but that doesn't stop the mad dash each spring to sign up for these programs, or the casual name-dropping that I hear around my community from parents who find out what I do. "My child is spending the summer at Stanford," one parent cooed to me as if she had discovered some secret path to admission.

The irony isn't lost on me or admissions officers that a summer camp with a hefty price tag and a designer label affixed to it is less valuable than a normal summer experience like a part-time job, community college course, or internship. Meaningful experiences lend themselves to meaningful growth and passion development, which lead to meaningful application essays, which ultimately contribute to a successful application more than "I spent two months living in a Stanford dorm recording videos for TikTok." Yet despite sharing this information with Taylor's parents and all families I work with so that they can invest their children's time and family's resources wisely, many parents who seek me out still sign their children up for these programs and brag to others in their community that their child is spending the summer at [insert fancy-name college here]. In the same breath, they explain that this college is their top choice and insinuate that their child's time on campus will make the case for admission to that school. I imagine that when the rejection from that college comes for their child, many interesting stories and explanations emerge to save face. But to these parents, it is worth paying $10,000 to brag that their child spent the summer at a glorified camp for teens from wealthy families.

That said, let's return to the story. The family was crushed because Taylor was rejected from the camp. Taylor, the eldest child, had never been rejected from *anything*. She was valedictorian of her middle school class, captain of her Science Olympiad team, and a perennial teacher's pet. Every teacher loved her and said she was by far the brightest student in her class. The fact that Harvard (but really, we are talking about a camp offered at Harvard) rejected her was beyond the pale. It was insulting, unfair, and flat-out wrong.

When it came time to start building a school list and application strategy, I asked Taylor what she was looking for.

"I like being surrounded by nature," she said. "I also really like the idea of a college town where life revolves around the school."

"That sounds great," I said. "There are lots of schools that would be good for nature and a college town feel. How about Dartmouth? Or Cornell?"

Taylor's parents were making faces at each other. Before I could get past Dartmouth and Cornell, they interrupted me. "We want her to apply early to Harvard."

"Of course, it's your decision," I said. "But have you visited Harvard before? If Taylor is looking for nature, I'm just not sure Cambridge is the place."

"It is Harvard," her mom said emphatically. Her dad nodded in distinct agreement. In fact, they were so certain that I left off any other suggestions and drew up a list with Harvard at the very top. Privately, though, I worried about Taylor and what would happen if the results didn't go her way. Yes, she had perfect grades and test scores, but that is not enough to earn admission to schools like Harvard, where most competitive applicants also have perfect grades and test scores.

In the end, she was not admitted to Harvard. Or Yale. Or Princeton. But she was admitted to Columbia, Brown, and Penn (all of which have below 5 percent acceptance rates, I might add). The parents were shocked, not because she was admitted to three Ivy League universities, but because she was rejected from their homemade acronym of "HYP."

Taylor enrolled at Columbia—in upper Manhattan—not because of its (lack of) access to nature or (lack of) a college town vibe on the Upper West Side, but simply because a Google search proved that it had the lowest acceptance rate of all her other options. Its low selectivity meant that Columbia had to be the best choice.

When Taylor's mom called to inform me of her daughter's decision, she was in tears. She was crushed by how unfair the process was. Her daughter would be attending a "low Ivy," and she simply didn't know how to cope since she firmly believed her daughter deserved to attend a "high Ivy."

As a graduate of Penn myself (a low Ivy, according to her classification), I wanted to tell her that there is no difference between a Columbia and a Harvard education. Economic theory and physics formulas remain the same, regardless of who is teaching them. Her daughter was simply unlucky and did not get accepted to Harvard but was lucky and accepted to Columbia.

But Taylor's mom and Taylor didn't agree with this. In my mind, she based her college decision on selectivity rather than fit. Columbia was not the right place for Taylor. She developed severe anxiety and chose to study economics simply because the economics program at Columbia is known for being one of the strongest programs at the school. It even required an additional application, which, to Taylor and her friend group, was interpreted as a symbol of its hyperselectivity and therefore desirability. Taylor kept chasing prestige in college and lost track of who she was and what she had originally hoped a college education would help her achieve.

While working on her economics program application, she confided in me that once she was admitted to the program, she would finally be able to relax and be happy. I asked her what she would focus on at that point, and she informed me that she wanted to find nature groups to join since nature was important to her. I tried to hide my confusion—nature, in New York City?—but it was clear to me that beyond Central Park, Taylor was clearly in the wrong environment. Blinded by her desire to collect accolades that looked good and would demonstrate her superiority above all others, she didn't know how to focus on achieving goals that would make her happy as well as accomplished.

When we blindly pursue being better than everyone else, we let being better than others trump what is best for us. In Taylor's case, anything less than Harvard, Yale, or Princeton was not the best and therefore not good enough. Attending Columbia, a university with incredible academic programs and experiences that may even exceed Harvard's, was inferior and imperfect in her eyes.

Studies have shown that "self-oriented perfectionism," defined as tying one's self-worth to achievement and being unable to derive a lasting sense of satisfaction from one's accomplishments, is rising among college students, with a 33 percent increase between 1989 and 2018.[26] "Socially prescribed perfectionism," defined as perfectionism that stems from a need to exceed high social expectations, is the most debilitating kind. Research has indicated that these unhealthy levels of perfectionism lead to increased suicidal tendencies, anxiety, disorders like anorexia, clinical perfectionism, and early death.[27] Living up to an unrealistic standard to "be the best" is hard to maintain, and this difficulty drives students to unsavory behaviors like cheating in order to uphold a perfect veneer. The irony is that when we must cheat, lie, or hedge in order to appear perfect, we are not really truly perfect anymore, are we?

Still, this debilitating fear of failing and damaging the "perfect" brand leads more than 79 percent of students surveyed across different high-performing high schools to admit to cheating in some way in the month prior to conducting the survey. The top two reasons are what they call "performance over mastery," where all they care about is getting the A, and "peer relationships / social comparison," where students are motivated by intense competition and a mindset of "cheat or be cheated" because everyone else is cheating.[28] For many students, it seems like the letter grade now matters much more than mastering the concepts or building the skills needed for long-term success.

In addition to cheating, which jeopardizes moral health, obsession with performance can lead students to risk their physical health. Many high school and college students illegally use prescription medication to help them study. Recent surveys found that almost 10 percent of college students have taken Adderall (prescription ADHD medication) to boost their academic performance. At the University of Michigan, 24 percent of those surveyed reported using Adderall to help them study.[29]

These habits can become long-term. In surveys about different professions and substance abuse, 9 percent of attorneys surveyed reported abusing prescription medication,[30] and a whopping 15 percent of doctors reported struggling with substance abuse.[31] While a JD or MD after any child's name may be the holy grail for a trophy-obsessed parent, we must be careful at the personal cost that comes to those who will stop at nothing to obtain it.

In an era when social media forces us to perpetually keep up with others who have experiences we covet or possessions we would love to own, parents can be the bulwark against a trophy-collecting mentality for their children. Parents must remind their children that what matters most is what makes them happy, not how others perceive them. Each person on this planet is running their own race. If the race speaks to them, their dreams, and their interests, regardless of the outcome, it is worth it. If it is spent chasing what others have, or achieving what others cannot achieve, what will be the destination?

Achievements exist to measure growth. While a fancy diploma hanging on the wall is what one receives after years of studying, the degree itself is not what propels a person to success or fulfillment. What lessons are learned along the way will. The skills and perspective are what candidates discuss in a job interview. Job applicants do not repeatedly recite where they went to school but rather the different things they learned that are relevant to an employer.

Young people should embrace prioritizing the experience, not the label that comes with it. This is easier said than done. To ensure that we stay focused on the experience, we must be open to reflection. Is what we are doing enjoyable? Do we feel we are on the right path? Is another path out there? These questions are tough for any person to answer, but especially for a young person who is easily influenced by peer pressure in a setting like high school or college, which inherently adds a degree of competition. Use the ends of school terms, school years, or natural ending points for activities as a chance to reflect upon the highlights and how the experience felt in the moment. Force the conversation to ensure that your young person is actually asking if they are on the right path. This may be the only way to hold them accountable to themselves and ensure that they focus on their passion rather than the false promise that accompanies a shiny trophy. Trophies fade and grow dull with time while the spark of passion continues to burn and light the way.

Helping a young person discover and develop their passion can be a process of trial and error. Parents can support their children by encouraging them to be honest with their interests and ensure that they set time aside for experiences that allow them to discover what inspires and excites them. Play the long game and encourage your children to focus on preparing for a sustainable and long-term path rather than short-term prestige.

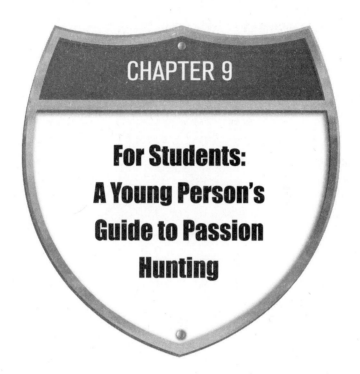

CHAPTER 9

For Students: A Young Person's Guide to Passion Hunting

GRIT IS THE TRAIT that allows you to overcome obstacles, and leadership is the cultivated skill that empowers you to make a difference, which is how you will be evaluated. But passion is what makes it all worth it for *you*. If you are passionate, you will inevitably be self-motivated to try a little harder, work a little longer, and find ways to innovate or make an impact. Passion is what propels you forward to live the life that you want. And for that reason, it may be the most important element of all.

There is no right or wrong passion to develop, as passions are unique to each of us. We may share similar passions with siblings, friends, and others, but there is no substitute for any individual's passions. For some, finding a passion comes easy or early in life. Others spend years dedicating themselves to causes or experiences that don't excite them.

One of the most frequent pieces of advice you will hear as a young person when it comes to your future is "Follow your passion." Part of the reason passion is stressed so much is that it is an internal motivator for working hard and sticking with a cause or activity even in challenging conditions. Without passion, it is easy to quit or not apply ourselves to the best of our abilities. In those trying times, that little extra something that passion contributes can make all the difference.

The advice about following passions comes from a good place but can be frustrating to hear when you don't know what your passions are. "Easier said than done" may feel like an appropriate response. Embrace that it is normal for a young person to not know their passions. Each of us must try new things and see what feels right. No matter how long it takes, we have to keep seeking until we find it.

Everyone's path to discovering and dedicating themselves to their passions should be as unique as each individual. Regardless of your interests, be intentional with how you spend your time and how you reflect upon whether your pursuits excite you. Play the long game and focus on what makes you happy now and could do so in the future. When it comes to college and even graduate school, maximize your odds that you will be able to follow your passions by crafting your education to fit your passions and not the other way around.

DO: Be honest with yourself.

Like anything else, developing and dedicating ourselves to our passion requires a lot of work—enjoyable work, but work nonetheless. First, landing on a passion demands honesty, especially at a young age when we are being pulled in different directions, trying to live up to familial or societal pressures, and without enough life experience to know what truly makes us happy. Understand that the journey may include false starts, twists, and turns. If we reflect on those moments in which an activity is not a fit, you can reflect upon what felt right and what didn't so that you can be more focused on what will excite you next time.

At every step, you need to be honest in order to ensure that you are making progress. Being honest with yourself forces you to be accountable when it comes to the effort needed to find your passion—so ask and frankly answer for yourself if you are committed to finding your passion, or are you just going through the motions. Finding our passion requires being intentional. We are asked to do many things that honestly don't excite us that much, such as homework, studying for class, or—for those who aren't musically inclined—practicing the piano. We have to do so many things every day that it is sometimes hard to make the time we need to explore new opportunities, see if we like them, and reflect on the experience to guide us for the future. We want to identify those that don't feel like chores even if a lot of daily activities need to be completed to put us in a position to find our passions.

Being intentional requires discipline. We must commit ourselves to having new experiences. This extends far beyond exploring something on the Internet or social media. It requires actually putting ourselves out there and seeing what it feels like. For some young people interested in health care as a career, volunteering at a hospital or health clinic is a possibility. Others who are interested in engineering can participate in programs like robotics or their local science fair. It is easy to discount something in theory, but each of us needs to have experiences to understand if we enjoy the responsibilities and tasks that accompany our passions.

Many new experiences and potential passions can seem overwhelming or daunting until we actually try them. The idea of coming up with an argument in a mock trial can seem intimidating, but working with other peers on the argument and delivering it in front of a judge may actually be fun in the moment. You need to have that experience to see for yourself. Until you try, you never know.

The journey may take time not just for the path to come but for each step along the way—*a lot of time*, in fact. We need to set aside the time to experiment with ourselves and see what sticks. If you find yourself stretched thin and lacking time, be honest and objective in evaluating your commitments so that you can prioritize the tasks, activities, and ideas that matter the most to you. You may find yourself longing to volunteer at a health clinic but lack the time. Where can you cut back? Does another activity bring you no joy or fulfillment? Your parents may think that being committed to an activity throughout your education may look good for colleges and career, but if it is leading you down a path where you don't want to go, is it worth it? Remind them (and yourself while you are at it) that you need to respond to these types of questions: *Why do I want to study in my intended field? Why do I want to study at [this specific] university? Why do I want to work here?* Giving yourself time to explore your passions offers you the chance to find the answers. The more experiences you have, the more persuasive these answers will be and the more direction you will have when it comes to choosing college or job possibilities.

Finally, when you have committed to spending the time that you need to explore and later develop your passions, ask yourself if you are willing to put in the work that it takes to make the most of your passion. While it feels exciting to be on our own journey, we need to do many things along the way that require a lot of work. Aspiring engineers need to master calculus and physics, for example. Not every test along the way will be enjoyable, but with passion as the North Star, it is easy for any young person to recognize that the effort they put in is what will prepare them for their futures.

Finding one's passion requires being honest about our experiences and what engages us. One student I worked with, Kyle, was told by his parents that he should become a computer programmer because he liked playing video games with his friends and because many of the most successful people in his tech-driven community worked as software engineers. When he enrolled in computer science classes at his high school, he procrastinated when doing his homework. He admitted he liked video games, but the social aspect with his friends was the best part.

Coding wasn't a passion for Kyle despite his competence and success in his related classes. I encouraged him to look inward and ask what he enjoyed in life. With reflection, he came to the conclusion that he was a people person and wanted to pursue a path that involved working with others. What that was, he didn't know, but he was committed to finding out.

Kyle applied to college with an undeclared major. He didn't want to lock himself into anything. His parents were nervous because they felt he had no direction. "Give him time," I cautioned them while reminding them that "as long as he is actively exploring, he will make progress." Kyle took different classes across the humanities, sciences, and arts but kept gravitating toward psychology classes that covered how to incentivize others to be the best version of themselves. He insisted he didn't want to become a psychologist but kept at it. He eventually participated in an internship the summer between his second and third years of college working in human resources and loved it. He admitted that his parents questioned why he would just want to push paper around and do administrative tasks. He explained that he would have the chance to help set a company's culture and work with employees to grow in their roles. Returning to college after his internship, Kyle declared a management major and became involved in business competitions for creating company work cultures. He even served as a research assistant for a professor studying employee retention methods. Upon graduating, he was hired by a large consulting firm where he is working alongside some of the largest companies in the world to create programs to develop their future talent.

Kyle is happy and more than financially independent. And Kyle will likely go much further in his career and life than had he just stuck to doing what people told him he should do. By committing during college to discovering what he enjoyed and then making time for what he was interested in, he landed on his path.

DON'T: Follow the herd.

Not only does following our passions take time. It can also take courage. Some people who are incredibly important to you will want to see you pursue what they think is best for you. Others may not fully understand your passions. Recognize that these people—whether they are family, friends, or trusted mentors—want the world for you.

But also acknowledge that they will not be the ones going through your life and living these experiences. While they can provide guidance and a sounding board, your passions are ultimately yours to live and explore.

Each of us needs to be honest about what makes us happy. This is not the same as what makes our parents happy or impresses others in our community. In those moments when we question the circumstances we face or the difficulties we encounter, we have to be able to rely strictly on our passion to propel us forward. If something is truly your passion, your progress and love for the subject will push you through self-doubt and allow you to reach the goals you've set.

Just as importantly, we all must recognize that others' paths aren't necessarily the right ones for us. Seeing others achieve incredible milestones on social media only intensifies the pressure and lays the trap to follow what is working for others. Just remember that there are no standards, set paths, or timelines for following our passions. Even those immersed in their passions and well on their way do not know where their journey will lead.

So when it comes to finding and following your passion, reflect on whether you are chasing what you want. Listen to friends, parents, classmates, and others in your community but chase your own passion. Yes, it is easy to be swayed, but stay true and authentic to who you are.

Some of the most impactful people in the world have pursued their interests to their benefit. Steve Jobs, as a college dropout, was fascinated by typography and calligraphy. He studied the art of different fonts while trying to figure out what made him tick as an individual. When launching Apple, he applied what he learned to the iconic Apple text that is a large part of the brand. It helped shape its quirky, less formal image that differentiated it from other PCs. He helped make Apple what it is today. People may have thought he was crazy in the moment, but following his interests, not those that belonged to others, molded him into the visionary he became.

One of my students, Ella, faced her own pressures to achieve. Growing up in a competitive community that placed a premium on where people go to college as a way to measure achievement, Ella initially wanted to go to NYU because it is a "prestigious college." In meetings, she admitted that NYU sounded good to her and she liked the idea of living in a place like New York City.

However, as she grew older, Ella's interests began to take form, and she grew interested in becoming a commercial pilot. When college admissions season came around, Ella was accepted to NYU, indeed a prestigious school that is both well known and fit perfectly with Ella's childhood dream. However, it is not the best fit for someone looking to study aeronautics and become a licensed pilot as part of their college education.

So Ella—*gasp!*—turned down NYU and attended Embry-Riddle Aeronautical University, which boasts one of the world's most celebrated and highly respected aeronautics programs. She also received an enormous scholarship and the chance to become a pilot instructor by her sophomore year of college. The strength of Embry-Riddle's aeronautics program ensured that, upon graduation, she would have many opportunities to begin a career in a field that speaks directly to her specific passions.

Soon-to-be-former friends mocked Ella for her decision. Their parents asked if she was crazy. But Ella was steadfast in her understanding of herself and what would make her happy. She cut ties with many of the doubters and found herself much closer to her college friends than her high school friends.

Ella is one of the happiest college students I have ever worked with. She has a clear-cut path to achieve her goals and is attending a college that is tailor-made for her specific interests. For the aspiring student pilot who stayed true to herself, both she and her parents may have had to endure snide remarks and raised eyebrows in her community about turning down admission to a selective institution. But Ella lived her life herself and not to impress others. She ultimately took advantage of her genuine passion to develop marketable skills that will ultimately give her an advantage in the job market. For icing on the cake, she is entering the commercial pilot job market, which is experiencing a critical shortage. Her earning potential is higher than many of her would-be classmates at NYU who are chasing bloated fields with heavy competition.

I share Ella's story as an example because it is so tempting to view our successes and progress through others' eyes. All we need to do is be honest about whether we are chasing what makes us happy and fulfilled. This requires staying true to ourselves and focusing on our own goals, not the validation we gain from other people. No one college has a monopoly on the path to success. No magic experiences will ensure that any of us are capable of achieving everything we want in the future. Life involves an incredible amount of trial and error. Skills, perspective, and passion can be acquired and developed through a myriad of different opportunities. By keeping an open mind, we can ensure that we have the experiences that will help us grow, even if we are unsure of where they may ultimately land us.

▉▉: Act upon your passions.

Once you identify your passions, you will need to find opportunities to transform them into a real and enduring foundation for your entire life. Passions need to be validated and tested. This is for your happiness, not just your future goals.

When it comes to picking classes in school, enroll in ones that you find intriguing. If advanced options exist, challenge yourself, if you feel comfortable, with the ones that capture your interest. Aspiring STEM students can push themselves in math and science classes, while those who enjoy history may find an advanced history or political science class more to their liking. Look to community colleges with summer school classes to gain exposure to fields that don't exist at your high school. While college admissions officers look favorably upon students who challenge themselves with these learning opportunities, this advice extends far beyond college admission. These classes will allow you to explore your interests in depth before applying to college to make sure the college you choose is a good fit for you.

Also, commit to finding ways to grow outside the classroom. Each person is more than a transcript. Admissions officers and employers place a premium on developing grit and leadership capabilities as well. Let your passions guide how you spend your time. High school students interested in coding can participate in hackathons or activities like Cyber Patriots, in which participants are tasked with identifying and reinforcing online vulnerabilities. Young people interested in foreign affairs and current events can join their high school's Model United Nations programs. If your school doesn't offer one, get online and see if your community has a club program.

Whatever your interests may be, dedicate yourself to them. You will develop a stronger understanding of who you are and what makes you tick. If you find that you do not enjoy something, incorporate that feedback into your plans and seek a new direction. There is no shame in a course correction, and when it comes to building a life plan, you can't make mistakes at an early age. Each false start or dead end eventually leads you closer to finding your long-term path.

Of all the students I have worked with, none demonstrated as much commitment to their passion as Skyler. Skyler loved race cars. As a kid, he enjoyed watching Formula One races with his parents and followed the sport religiously. Along the way many people told him to find another passion and that he was never going to grow up to be a race car driver. Yes, being a professional race car driver is rare, but that doesn't mean Skyler couldn't stay true to his love of racing and pursue it as a career.

In high school, Skyler joined his high school's robotics team and built the drivetrain for the robot. He learned the fundamentals of vehicle design and saw a way to apply his love of racing as an engineer. When the time came to start looking into colleges, Skyler was committed to finding ways to apply his passion for racing. Rather than applying to mechanical engineering programs, Skyler researched programs online that were more tailored to racing and discovered a few in Europe and Australia that were well suited for people with passions like his. He ended up applying to and enrolling in a university in Europe that cost less than an American university but set him up for a job on a Formula One team as an engineer.

Skyler allowed his passions to steer him through all aspects of his life. He landed his dream job because he stayed committed to his dreams every step of the way. You can also lean into your interests, whatever they may be. Your life will reward you for finding ways to incorporate them into everything you do. Whether that is as a person with a love of storytelling becoming a filmmaker creating visual campaigns as a marketer, or someone who loves building things as an engineer, do not lose sight of the experiences you have that bring you joy. You will be happier if you find ways to make life fit your goals. Do not fall into the trap of allowing others' goals to shape your life. Spend your time wisely by focusing on the things you love to do. You will enjoy each step of the journey much more along the way.

DON'T: Spend more on college than your passion can afford.

While passions come from within and need not cost anything, being able to pursue them can be difficult or impossible if you are not in a financial position to chase your dreams. Today, seven in ten students graduate college with loans. At the end of 2022, a whopping 43.5 million Americans held over $1.6 trillion in student loans. The average borrower with student loans holds a balance of over $37,000.

Imagine that you have a budding passion for entrepreneurship and want to start the next revolutionary tech company that you believe will become wildly successful. There is only one problem: In the first few years, you may not be able to afford to pay yourself much of a salary to cover your living expenses as you grind to get your business off the ground, and you may have to reinvest back in the business what it earns to help it grow. It would be impossible to pursue this dream if you take out tens or hundreds of thousands of dollars of student loans to finance your education and are required to make a hefty repayment each month. You'll feel pressure to work a job to pay your obligations (aka bills). Or you may dream of becoming a designer; however, many creative fields offer low starting salaries as you learn the tricks of the trade.

If you can't afford to pay for your housing and student loan payments, you may find it impossible to follow your passions and build the skill set to empower your future success. Again, like the aspiring entrepreneur, you may be forced to settle for doing something else that is not your passion. It happens all the time with people. In fact, half of student loan borrowers report that their student loans affect their career choices.[32] We want to avoid these situations. Aside from not being able to chase their dreams, student loans are one of the most often cited reasons that Millennials and Gen Zers report as reasons that they are living at home with their parents rather than buying homes, getting married, or starting their own families. Whatever your dreams are, professionally and personally, student loans will make it harder for you to live the life you want.

It can be challenging to set and stick to an educational budget. Each person has different financial circumstances. Just because some people can afford to go to an expensive private university without scholarships doesn't mean that it is the right place for you if you will need to finance your education with student loans. Today, private universities may cost more than $90,000 per year without scholarships or financial aid. Over four years, the total cost may be more expensive than many homes.

If the education and potential debt are worth it to you, there is nothing wrong with taking out massive student loans to pay for college. Just make an informed decision when it comes to the debt, what the balance will be with interest, and how you expect to pay for it after you graduate, based on your career goals. It is important to be honest when it comes to repayment ability. Many of my law school classmates who expected to be making more than $100,000 per year as new attorneys were confronted with the harsh truth that the *average* starting salary for a lawyer in private practice is $56,000 per year. Many of them reported that they would not have picked our law school and financed their education with loans if they had known this before they committed to going there or to law school in general. Yet they only have themselves to blame as this information is readily available. Learn from these common mistakes when developing your own educational path.

It is rational to treat higher education like an investment that helps you reach your goals. You can overpay for your education if you exceed your budget. Stick with your budget and give yourself the financial freedom to pursue your dreams. Apply to universities that offer generous merit scholarships for students with similar academic profiles. Some colleges even offer full-tuition scholarships for students who meet certain GPA and test score thresholds.

You can also start your higher education at a community college. In many states, tuition is free or low-cost. Not only will you save tens of thousands of dollars on tuition, but you will also save on living costs for the first few years if you stay at home. Many universities, including the prestigious University of California system, offer guaranteed transfer admission programs for meeting GPA requirements. These universities also strive to create social experiences that support transfer students by encouraging them to get involved in social organizations like clubs and even fraternities and sororities.

Moreover, you will not miss out on the social college experience by starting at a community college. You will merely delay it from age eighteen to twenty, which isn't that big a deal in the grand scheme of things. Just remember, by living within your means, you will still be able to reach your college milestones. It may come later than expected, but if it allows you to chase your dreams, it could be worth it.

Treat college as a chance to grow and prepare for your future. Yes, this involves making new friends and having new social experiences, but not at the expense of burdening your entire adult life with debt to the point that you cannot live the life that a college education should bring you closer to attaining.

By balancing your aspirations with realistic goals, you will achieve much more than what you initially expect. One of my students, Ali, came to me with dreams of becoming a doctor. She was concerned about the cost of her entire education because, on top of college, medical school can cost from $50,000 to $100,000 per year when factoring in tuition and living expenses. Many of her friends were applying to expensive private universities, and she felt that she was going to be left behind. I encouraged Ali to play the long game and stay focused on her goals. I reminded her that it was more important to be in a position to go to med school than fall victim to the social media craze surrounding college admission and apply to schools she couldn't afford to attend. She committed to applying to only public universities in her home state of California. There was only one problem: Many of the UC schools she applied to had very low acceptance rates. Ali was not admitted to a UC campus she wanted to attend, so—playing the long game—she decided to stay home, enroll at a local community college, and knock out her required general education classes. Ali was worried about missing out on all the fun and the excitement, but she found ways to stay socially active and engaged. Was she craving something new? Yes. But she eventually got there.

After two years, Ali had a stellar GPA and earned admission to her initial top-choice college: University of California, Santa Barbara. She knew that she would have to put in work to make friends when she transferred, but she was willing to do that so that she could chase her goals after college. She lived with other transfer students in a house near the beach and applied to medical school after graduation. Her student loan levels were minimal, and she will be able to manage her medical school loans since she doesn't have to worry about a heavy undergraduate debt burden.

The beautiful thing about following one's passion rather than prestige is that it can help you find the right educational path that makes sense for you. Remember, no college has a monopoly on the path to success. While some schools may be considered more prestigious than others, ask yourself, *Where does this prestige come from, and will that prestige help me achieve my goals? Is there a lower-cost alternative to help me reach my potential?* Even if you do not receive the same level of support at a local public college or university, you can still achieve your goals. You may have to work harder or network on your own, but the cost savings may ultimately prove to be the factor that allows you to actually do what you want.

With graduate degrees, it is also important to be flexible and assess the financial outcomes as some paths may require less expensive and less stressful educations that ultimately fit your goals better. Many aspiring healthcare providers think they need to go to medical school to be financially successful. However, many nurse practitioners and other nurses with advanced degrees earn higher salaries in specialized medical fields than general practitioner medical doctors. As with college and graduate school, be committed to living the type of life you want and make your education and career path fit that. You should not have to bend your goals to pursue paths that do not make sense to you.

Passion hunting, like anything else, takes work. You need to be honest and willing to throw yourself into meaningful experiences to find out what works best for you. In the end, your work now will pay off in the future—when your work is fulfilling, enjoyable, and made interesting by all the experience and knowledge you gain now. It also requires you to be honest with yourself so that you can avoid the false promise of other people's passions. You want to be fully available when you find the passion that suits you. The skills and perspective you gain in your search for it will allow you to make the most of your passion when you find it.

FINAL THOUGHTS ON PASSION

WHATEVER YOUR PASSIONS MAY BE, commit to finding and developing them. "Passion" is one of those buzzwords that is thrown around incessantly, for good reason. Passion is what excites us and inspires us to dedicate ourselves to our pursuits. It is the special sauce that makes the effort, struggles, and sacrifices worth it, capturing our imagination and motivating us to seize the day every day. No one wants a young person to dedicate themselves to pursuits that lack meaning or purpose. While each of us is required to do many things we do not want to do, passion is an important guide because it can allow us to filter through the many experiences that compete for our attention but do not lead to our fulfillment.

Parents, orient your child's development to discovering and growing in their passion. Remember, one's passion comes from within. While parents can help guide and steer a young person to fulfillment, they need to provide their child the space to be authentic to what that is. Providing the space and support children need to develop their passions will be the greatest gift parents can offer.

A young person can make the most of this gift by giving themselves the time they need to discover their passions. Young people must be honest with themselves and reflect on whether their pursuits actually excite them. When they discover their passions, commit your child to building them into a sustainable and enduring foundation for a journey that is as meaningful and enjoyable as reaching the intended destination.

CONCLUSION

● ● ●

IT IS NEVER TOO LATE
TO BE WHAT YOU MIGHT HAVE BEEN.

—GEORGE ELIOT

THIS IS THE END OF THE BOOK, but it's just another step in your continuing journey, even as destinations and people change along the way. What will remain the same, regardless of where we are headed, is the need to prepare ourselves to seize every opportunity that comes our way.

PARENTS: Your journey is evolving as you grow from the person responsible for the health and happiness of your child to the sounding board, confidant, and cheerleader for a young person to define what happiness is for them and the path to achieve it. All you can ask of yourselves or your children is to focus on the journey and improve a little bit every day. Parents and their children alike need to find new ways to grow by leaning into what makes them tick and finding ways to make an impact.

This requires thinking beyond the now. It's a difficult habit to break, especially since it is only natural to want the best for our children ever since their birth. It may be agonizing to have to restrain yourself from stepping in and fixing everything to ensure your child's success. You may feel like the rest of your child's life depends on their performance in high school and the outcome of the college admissions process. But a parent's responsibility is to focus on the long game and prepare their children for what lies ahead. The best way anyone can support their children is to help them develop into healthy, happy, and financially independent adults who are capable of contributing to society. Too many adults today never grow up.

STUDENTS: This journey requires you to be intentional with how you grow. It will reward you for following your heart and balancing your dreams with the world's practical realities so that you can find your way in it. You need to try new things, commit yourself to your passions, and along the way, develop the grit and leadership skills required to apply yourself to succeed. This is your race to run and yours alone.

As a college counselor, I have the privilege of seeing students enter my office, unsure of themselves or their place in the world, and—within the span of a few short years—grow into human beings who demonstrate the potential to make an impact on the world. At the end of high school, they usually have even racked up accomplishments in the form of incredible college options. With this in mind, I say, students: life will reward you for making the most of what is to come. Every opportunity presented to you will be a learning lesson.

Regardless of the outcomes, what you learn, how you grow, and how it shapes your future actions will determine your path and future success. Lean into the experiences and embrace the discomfort as it arises, because the experiences and discomfort will help shape you into the person you are meant to be.

We began this book with the story of life being over for a student who lacked perspective regarding not being admitted to (*gasp!*) Stanford. This book is a rejection of that thought and an invitation for each young person to make the most of their journey. The world young people will inherit in the coming years may look very different than it does today. Technological advancements, climate change, and many other factors will present challenges, but also incredible opportunities, for young people to apply themselves to solve problems and innovate. It is up to them to seize these opportunities and make them work for themselves.

Therefore, rather than focusing on rigid paths, embrace that the journey will include many twists and turns. Achieving success throughout it will simply require being prepared. What does this mean? Navigating the journey will call on young people to develop and apply their grit, their ability to lead, and their passion to the circumstances they face. Young people need to equip themselves with these skills and the perspective to harness the journey so that it leads them to health, happiness, and financial independence. Along the way, they should stay true to who they are by prioritizing their well-being and gaining the skills needed to do the things they desire.

To conclude this book, I want to share three short stories of students I have worked with whose grit, leadership, and passion have propelled them to success in high school, college, and beyond. They have served as the inspiration for my desire to write this book. I have shared many stories of success and shortcomings, but with each of these three, I speak not just as a college admissions adviser but as an entrepreneur and employer who was so impressed by who they are that I asked them to work for me after they graduated from high school.

Grit: Julia

I met Julia when she was a sophomore in high school. Julia thought high school would be a lot more relaxed than it turned out for her, as she worked many hours to help with her family's finances. She balanced a few part-time jobs and was constantly hustling for babysitting gigs and tutoring opportunities with her younger brother's friends. Her family had endured some personal trauma, which led her to go to therapy—which in turn prompted Julia to become very interested in finding ways to improve her mental health.

I encouraged Julia to apply the grit she had gained through life to help others, which she was glad to do. She started a mental health organization at her high school and even self-published a fictionalized account of her struggles to let other teens know they are not alone. She turned the lessons she learned into a way to help others.

When the time came to apply to college, Julia wrote not about what she had endured personally but the satisfaction she gained from helping others work through their own challenges. She was admitted to University of California, Berkeley, which is considered one of the top public universities in the country. But cognizant of her family's financial struggles, she ultimately enrolled at Tulane because she received a generous scholarship that covered almost all her tuition.

Julia's story did not end there. Having heard over the years about all the unpleasantness she dealt with working at an ice cream shop, restaurant, and cafe and the Karens for which her hometown is known, I knew that Julia had grit. She had no fear of rejection, challenging situations, or difficult people. So I asked her to help with marketing and partnership outreach for an online platform I built to assist students in navigating the college admissions process.

Julia is now studying for the LSAT and applying to law school. Her goal is to obtain a large merit scholarship and help people resolve their challenges through the legal system. She has a genuine passion for helping others and the grit needed to deal with tough situations to reach her goals. Julia knows how to live within her means and will be a healthy, happy, and financially independent adult. She is a true embodiment of grit and how it can lead to a fulfilling path.

Leadership: Sean

I met Sean at the end of his junior year of high school. He was stressed about applying to college and worried that he hadn't done enough in high school. He asked if it was okay that he didn't play a sport or serve on his school's student council. Sean was outspoken in class but shied away from school activities that felt like popularity contests. He was passionate about politics and international affairs, especially regarding the Middle East, from where his family had emigrated. Because he wanted to make a difference, Sean organized debates about the crisis in Syria to educate his peers and correct misconceptions about people in the Middle East. I was impressed with Sean's courage to bring his classmates together despite the racist insults some hurled at him. I saw a young person developing conviction in himself and a plan to change people's minds—someone committed to making an impact.

Sean built his college application around these debates and wrote about what he learned about his community. He composed an essay about his desire to have civil discourse and correct misinformation. He was admitted to his dream school—UCLA—despite having slightly lower grades and SAT scores than some of his competitors. When he graduated, Sean gained employment at a consulting firm where he works on teams that advise large companies on how to improve their operations. The lessons he learned in high school about making an impact on his community have applied to his career, and he is now paid to help companies grow.

Sean's success in high school prepared him for his future. There were no corners to cut. His growth as a leader is what sustains him as a professional. Sean is also well on his way to health, happiness, and financial independence.

Passion: Maxine

Maxine loves to write. When I met her and she shared her writing with me for the first time, I didn't think she would need much help on the college applications other than brainstorming ideas. Maxine wrote for her school magazine and her community newspaper, and also entered writing competitions. Her passion was hard to hide.

Maxine was proud of the fact that she quit activities along the way that she didn't find meaningful. She took the time she spent on sports that no longer served her and reinvested it into activities where she had the potential to achieve leadership positions, such as the school magazine, where she served as editor-in-chief for two years running. The summer before her senior year, Maxine was accepted to a program where she served as a research assistant for a graduate student writing a thesis about the role of propaganda in the

Cold War. She was able to channel her love of writing with another one of her interests: international affairs.

Maxine had plenty to write about when the time came to apply to college. She is now an English major at the University of Southern California. She is also taking accounting courses and interning at an asset valuation firm during the school year and summer.

Since graduating from high school, she has served as the writing assistant for this book. Maxine is someone I am so grateful to know and work with because her passion propels me forward as an individual and helps to motivate the organization that I lead. Maxine is proof that passion, when combined with grit and leadership, can lead to incredible opportunities.

These students serve as examples not as a point of comparison but as proof that it can be done—young people can launch themselves. Our hope for a better world lies with these dedicated young people and the countless others who are growing and preparing to make the most of their journeys. Despite the ominous statistics about financial instability and mental health struggles, young people continue to work hard and launch their brilliant futures.

You can do this too. You just need to create your own path that speaks to who you are and would like to be. Develop a plan to harness your potential and all that the journey has to offer. Discover and enrich your unique ability to add value to the journey—not just for yourself but for others. Each of us will be rewarded with fulfillment and in other ways we cannot even begin to contemplate. Grit, leadership, and passion will ebb and flow throughout a young person's development. Do not force any of them along the way. Simply be mindful of opportunities to discover who you are and what inspires you. There are no right or wrong opportunities to grow. Even if it is a false start or a dead end, the lessons can be applied to the journey to come.

Similarly, recognize once again that no college or career path offers a monopoly on the road to success. As I've said, more San Jose State graduates are working in Silicon Valley than Stanford grads. Perhaps the student featured at the beginning of this book who thought her life was over should reframe her perspective and focus on more important things: career, health, fulfillment, and happiness.

Each of us at times may need to make a 180-degree turn on the journey. Twists and turns are to be expected. Smooth sailing the entire way would be comfortable but probably not lead any of us to appreciate how much growth occurs on our individual journeys. In my own life, I never thought I would be writing this book or have a career that would warrant it. Burning out in investment banking and crying at the office alone on Thanksgiving made me realize that prestige matters little in the grand scheme of things. Finding that the practice of law was not for me is what prompted me to reflect upon what does make me happy—helping people—and finding a way to do just that.

If I wasn't tested along the way, I do not know if I could help prepare others for the challenges that await them. But the unforeseen avenues each of us have in the future are what make life so rewarding and interesting. None of us knows what is in store—and quite frankly, I wouldn't have it any other way. I hope for nothing more when it comes to young people than for them to have an open mind and the skills and perspective they need to seize life's opportunities as they arise. The journey will transform them into who they are meant to be.

You may feel alone sometimes. Find what makes you happy—your passion. It will bring you in contact with others with shared views of the world and similar goals. Do not settle for other people's passions. Your true passion will lead you to a brilliant future. You may feel unprepared, with shaky steps at times. This is normal. Gain the skills that you need to succeed in the long term. Be a leader when it's appropriate, and rely on your grit to stay the course and move forward.

Parents need to exercise patience with themselves and their children. Be kind to yourself and your teenager. Our entire lives are the journey, and things sometimes take longer than we would hope. There is no need to rush what will be a lifetime of experiences that will strengthen you and provide you with color, depth, and a sense of appreciation for each step and the path itself.

Your journey will transform you not only into who you are meant to be, but also into the best version of yourself: A person who is prepared for a changing and competitive world and on the path to health, happiness, and financial independence.

To your journey!

NOTES

● ● ●

1. Pew Research Center, "The Boomerang Generation: Feeling OK About Living with Mom and Dad," March 15, 2012, https://www.pewresearch.org/social-trends/2012/03/15/the-boomerang-generation/."

2. National Collegiate Athletic Association, "Estimated Probability of Competing in College Athletics," updated April 8, 2020, https://www.ncaa.org/sports/2015/3/2/estimated-probability-of-competing-in-college-athletics.aspx.

3. National Federation of State High School Associations, "NCAA Recruiting Facts," accessed September 26, 2023, https://www.nfhs.org/media/886012/recruiting-fact-sheet-web.pdf.

4. Angela L. Duckworth, Christopher Peterson, Michael D. Matthews, and Dennis R. Kelly, "Grit: Perseverance and Passion for Long-Term Goals," *Journal of Personality and Social Psychology* 92, no. 6 (June 2007): 1087–101, doi: 10.1037/0022-3514.92.6.1087.

5. Katherine R. Von Culin, Eli Tsukayama, and Angela L. Duckworth, "Unpacking Grit: Motivational Correlates of Perseverance and Passion for Long-Term Goals," *Journal of Positive Psychology* 9, no. 4 (2014): 306–12, doi: 10.1080/17439760.2014.898320.

6. Kamlesh Singh and Shalini Duggal Jha, "Positive and Negative Affect, and Grit as Predictors of Happiness and Life Satisfaction," *Journal of the Indian Academy of Applied Psychology* 34 (January 2008): 40–45, https://www.researchgate.net/publication/285749956_Positive_and_negative_affect_and_grit_as_predictors_of_happiness_and_life_satisfaction.

7. Claire Cain Miller and Jonah E. Bromwich, "How Parents Are Robbing Children of Adulthood," *New York Times,* March 16, 2019, https://www.nytimes.com/2019/03/16/style/snowplow-parenting-scandal.html.

8. Jennifer Ludden, "Helicopter Parents Hover in the Workplace," NPR, February 6, 2012, https:/www.npr.org/2012/02/06/146464665/helicopter-parents-hover-in-the-workplace.

9. Arti Patel, "'Snowplow Parenting' Is Preventing Young Adults from Learning 'Basic Life Skills,'" *Global News,* March 21, 2019, https://globalnews.ca/news/5076459/snowplow-parenting-problems/.

10. Ludden, "Helicopter Parents Hover in the Workplace."

11. Common Data Set Initiative, https://commondataset.org/.

12. International Center for Academic Integrity, "Facts and Statistics," accessed September 26, 2023, https://academicintegrity.org/resources/facts-and-statistics.

13. Nick Barney and Mary K. Pratt, "What Is Leadership?," TechTarget|CIO, updated March 2023, https://www.techtarget.com/searchcio/definition/leadership.

14. Jean M. Twenge, Jonathan Haidt, Andrew B. Blake, Cooper McAllister, Hannah Lemon, and Astrid Le Roy, "Worldwide Increases in Adolescent Loneliness," *Journal of Adolescence* 93 (December 2021): 257–69, https://www.sciencedirect.com/science/article/pii/S0140197121000853.

15. Trent Nguyen and Susan Landau, "Effects of Gaming on Children's Brains: Depression and Social Isolation," *Advances in Social Sciences Research Journal* 6, no. 9 (2019): *291–302*, https://doi.org/10.14738/assrj.69.4856.

16. "25 Surprising Leadership Statistics to Take Note of (2022)," Apollo Technical, May 25, 2022, https://www.apollotechnical.com/leadership-statistics/.

17. Kathleen Smith, "6 Common Triggers of Teen Stress," Psycom, updated October 21, 2022, https://www.psycom.net/common-triggers-teen-stress.

18. Dana Wilkie, "Employers Say Students Aren't Learning Soft Skills in College: Part 2: College Grads Are Deficient in Critical Thinking, Teamwork, Speaking and Writing, Executives Say," SHRM, October 21, 2019, https://www.shrm.org/resourcesandtools/hr-topics/employee-relations/pages/employers-say-students-arent-learning-soft-skills-in-college.aspx.

19. Ibid.

20. Amy Morin and Claire Gillespie, "What Americans of All Ages Are Worrying About Right Now, from the Silent Generation to Gen Z," Verywell Mind, October 8, 2021, https://www.verywellmind.com/what-americans-of-all-ages-are-worrying-about-right-now-5202028.

21. H. Sigmundsson, B. H. Dybendal, J. M. Loftesnes, B. Ólafsson, and S. Grassini, "Passion a Key for Success: Exploring Motivational Factors in Football Players," *New Ideas in Psychology* 65 (April 2022): 100932, https://doi.org/10.1016/j.newideapsych.2022.100932.

22. Bridget Shirvell, "How Much Should Parents Influence Their Kid's Career Choice?," updated January 18, 2023, *Parents,* https://www.parents.com/kids/development/parents-can-have-a-big-influence-on-their-kids-career-choice-but-thats-not-always-a-good-thing/.

23. Jay Atkinson, "How Parents Are Ruining Youth Sports: Adults Should Remember What Athletics Are Really About," *Boston Globe,* May 4, 2014, https://www.bostonglobe.com/magazine/2014/05/03/how-parents-are-ruining-youth-sports/.

24. Angela Lumpkin and Judy Favor, "Comparing the Academic Performance of High School Athletes and Non-athletes in Kansas in 2008–2009," *Journal of Sport Administration & Supervision* 4, no. 1 (March 2012): 41–62, http://hdl.handle.net/2027/spo.6776111.0004.108.

25. Noelle R. Leonard, Marya V. Gwadz, Amanda Ritchie, Jessica L. Linick, Charles M. Cleland, Luther Elliott, and Michele Grethel, "A Multi-method Exploratory Study of Stress, Coping, and Substance Use Among High School Youth in Private Schools," *Frontiers in Psychology* 6 (July 23, 2015): 1028, doi: 10.3389/fpsyg.2015.01028.

26. Jane Adams, "More College Students Seem to Be Majoring in Perfectionism," *New York Times,* January 18, 2018,

https://www.nytimes.com/2018/01/18/well/family/more-college-students-seem-to-be-majoring-in-perfectionism.html.

27. Thomas Curran and Andrew P. Hill, "Perfectionism Is Increasing over Time: A Meta-analysis of Birth Cohort Differences from 1989 to 2016," *Psychological Bulletin* 145, no. 4 (2019): 410–29, http://dx.doi.org/10.1037/bul0000138.

28. Samantha Selby, "Insights into How & Why Students Cheat at High Performing Schools," Challenge Success, March 24, 2019, https://challengesuccess.org/resources/insights-into-how-why -students-cheat-at-high-performing-schools/.

29. Ashley Addiction Treatment, "College Student Drug Use Statistics," accessed September 26, 2023, https://www.ashleytreatment .org/college-student-drug-use-statistics/.

30. Priscilla Henson, "Addiction & Substance Abuse in Lawyers: Statistics to Know," American Addiction Centers, updated September 12, 2023, https://americanaddictioncenters.org /rehab-guide/workforce/white-collar/lawyers.

31. Courtney Barber, "Drug and Alcohol Rehab for Doctors near Me," American Addiction Centers, updated May 17, 2023, https://americanaddictioncenters.org/healthcare-professionals /rehab-for-doctors

32. Annie Nova, "How Student Loans Are Making Some People Abandon Their Dreams," CNBC, July 18, 2018, https://www .cnbc.com/2018/07/17/how-student-loans-are-making-some -people-abandon-their-dreams.html.

ACKNOWLEDGMENTS

• • •

MY JOURNEY TO WRITE THIS BOOK would not have been possible without the support from those who have pushed me to make the most of every opportunity. This is a dream come true for the fully grown version of a seventeen-year-old rejected from the creative writing program at his dream school (Princeton). Studying finance at Wharton, working as a banker, burning out, going to law school, realizing that wasn't right for me either, and then finally forging the opportunity to work with students allowed me to discover my voice and a reason to use it.

Immense thanks are due to Mel Berger, my agent at William Morris Endeavor. His sage advice and advocacy on my behalf were monumental. I am also thankful to my editor at HCI, Darcie Abbene, for refining my voice and guiding me to stay true to the meaning of my words.

I am grateful to work with a team at Kaplan Educational Group whose commitment to the students we serve is at the core of their being. Their laughs make this journey enjoyable. I am thankful for them being with me every step of the way.

Words cannot adequately capture the gratitude I have for Maxine, one of the exemplars in the conclusion of this book. This book would not exist without her. She is living proof that the journey we are on is more fulfilling when shared with true friends that allow each of us to shine.

ABOUT THE AUTHOR

· · ·

GREG KAPLAN is an internationally recognized college admissions strategist and speaker. Headquartered in Newport Beach, his firm, the Kaplan Educational Group, helps hundreds of high school seniors and more than a thousand underclassmen reach their educational and career potential each year. Greg is a graduate of the Wharton School of the University of Pennsylvania and the UC Irvine School of Law, where he received close to a full-tuition scholarship. Greg draws on his experience as an investment banker and lawyer to tie one's education to long-term goals. Beyond earning admission, Greg and the Kaplan Educational Group team are committed to helping all their students become healthy, happy, and financially independent adults. To learn more about academic and career consulting services, visit kaplaneducationalgroup.com.